Mobil Travel Guide

il Travel Guide, the largest selling guide in the world.

"When she returned to their table a [...] the open-air restaurant in Napeague.

WHITE NINJA
by Eric Lustbader

LOBSTER ROLL, THE/LUNCH

Newsday

Peter M. Gianotti,
DINING OUT WITH NEWSDAY/99.
"The Lobster Roll embodies summertime eating: casual, light, fun, right for the whole family. It's a citadel of fresh, East End seafood simply prepared and enjoyable."

Eating Out East '89 - "Lobster Roll, Mtk. Hwy. on the Napeague Stretch, has one of the best values in the Hamptons area...its lobster roll, an outstanding seller since 1965..."

...r - "Lobster Roll does not disappoint. The Lobster salad is worthy of the words that have been devoted to it up until now... The breading on the soft shell crabs so crisp it's an experience to eating fresh, hot, ...made potato chips..." The ...bster Roll is a ...classic. ...does

INSIDERS RESORT GUIDE · PAGE 7

GRANNY POOH'S BEST!
Lobster Roll, THE/LUNCH is still far and away the best of the "beach" restaurants that dot the strip of Montauk Highway between Amagansett and downtown Montauk. It bustles and hustles and you'll feel most comfortable with a t-shirt and shorts on and a few kids in tow.

IN STYLE MAGAZINE
"The Lobster Roll (affectionately known as LUNCH because of the big LUNCH sign outside) has become the one eatery to which every visitor to the eastern-most tip of Long Island must pay homage..."

COUNTRY MAGAZINE
"World renowned lobster salad roll and other seafood favorites..."

LONG ISLAND UPDATE.
"One of the East Ends most popular dining spots and an absolute must-stop."

EAT YOUR WAY ACROSS THE U.S.A.
"The Lobster Roll is one of the essential seafood shacks in the Hamptons that has been here forever."

Joan Reminick, EXPLORING LONG ISLAND WITH NEWDAY
"Justly renowned for its world-famous lobster roll, this wildly popular seafood stop offers lots more."

More Celebrity Quotes

Great Place! - Secretary of State Madeline Albright
A Great Restaurant - President Richard Nixon
Cheers!- Billy Joel & Cristie Brinkley
Thank You! - Barbra Streisand
Delicious! - Bernadette Peters
A Great Place - Beau Bridges
Yummy! - Robert Klein
Great - Rick Moranis

HAMPTON'S MAGAZINE - RESTAURANT NOTES
Lobster Roll, Amagansett
A rainy Hamptons weekend as so many of us have seen this summer. A drive is the decision... and taken a step further: the decision is made to **LUNCH** at the Lobster Roll. You can't miss the sign. In case you haven't done it yet, this is the scene. The wet road to Montauk is long. It is oceanside and so you might associate it with sunshine. But sitting in the little understated enclosure, the air so thick and wet The feeling in this place is unlike any the Hamptons has to offer. that the road was barely visible, the sound of the rain and the thundering waves... **LUNCH** on the rainy day was enough to make the whole weekend.

DAN'S PAPERS - DINING IN THE HAMPTONS by Florence Kullick
Lobster Roll, Rte. 27 at Napeague Beach
Those of us who live out here for real, know how to tell the [...] known as **LUNCH**, (cause the sign says so) has opene[...]
All of the young, energetic staff scoot around in the[...]
the patrons happy.

Lobster Roll is neither Glitz nor Ritz. It [...]
know that this is a place for tempting[...]
service and substantial portions[...]
LUNCH. Alec Baldwin an[...]
Pele, Cheryl Tiegs, Ke[...]

...d Fred Terry and ...rve as **Professors** ...agement during ...y have 9 college ...also helps direct ...al Boards of the ...e Restaurant ...a and Paul have ...taurant training ...or years, have a ...minar company, ...eynote speakers ...the National ...ion. They have

It's on the placemat...and it's very impressive! Of course, it doesn't tell you about how all winter long, recipes are being tested in culinary labs, or how they pioneered Lobster Rolls in the area, were the first to offer Marinated Charbroiled fish, Cockles and Mussels, Seafood Caesar, Pecan Sole, Shrimp Rockefeller, Puffers Tempura, Huckleberry Pie, and in more recent years...Swordfish, Tuna, & Salmon burgers which everybody is going to copy...cause they're *soooooooo* good! Even Gourmet

the lobster roll

the lobster roll

and other pleasures
of summer by the beach

FROM THE FAMED HAMPTONS RESTAURANT KNOWN AS "LUNCH"

jodi della femina and andrea terry

PHOTOGRAPHS BY BEN FINK

clarkson potter/publishers
new york

Published by Clarkson Potter/Publishers, New York, New York
Member of the Crown Publishing Group, a division of Random House, Inc.
www.randomhouse.com

CLARKSON N. POTTER is a trademark and POTTER and colophon are registered
trademarks of Random House, Inc.

Printed in Singapore

Design by Jane Treuhaft

Library of Congress Cataloging-in-Publication Data
Della Femina, Jodi.
The lobster roll (and other pleasures of summer by the beach): from the famed
Hamptons restaurant known as "Lunch" / Jodi Della Femina and Andrea Terry;
photographs by Ben Fink.
1. Cookery. 2. Cookery (Seafood) 3. Lobster Roll (Restaurant) I. Terry, Andrea.
II. Title.
TX714.D445 2003
641.5—dc21   2002032967

ISBN 1-4000-4584-3

10 9 8 7 6 5 4 3 2 1

First Edition

for John and Carl—

thanks

for your unending support and
your bottomless appetites!

contents

welcome to "lunch"

The South Fork of Long Island, or the Hamptons, as the area is more commonly known, has always been a tremendous part of our lives. It's hard to explain the energy and excitement that fill the air when the farm stands open in April, their wooden bins stocked with fresh, delicious produce. The days get longer, the ocean begins to change color, and the air smells like summer is once again on its way.

Everyone has his or her favorite way to celebrate the coming season. For us, it's preparing a delicious meal with the many flavors the area has to offer. We both love certain farm stands that we can't wait to see back in operation—places we'll visit countless times for sweet juicy peaches, crunchy yellow and white corn, deep green chives, ruby-red strawberries that fill the air with the smell of natural sugar, enormous red tomatoes that are so tasty you can

eat them like an apple, and, of course, such treats as fruit crumbles, jellies, and jams.

Firing up the grill for the season's first barbecue, digging a hole in the sand for the inaugural bonfire (complete with s'mores), sipping that first summer cocktail as the sun begins to drop, rinsing the sand off your feet after walking up wooden stairs that have softened from the weather, hearing the crash of waves as you fall into a late-afternoon slumber, a dusting of salt on your skin and hair . . . this is summer on the East End, a true state of mind.

If summer were a place you could visit, your friends and family in tow, you would find it midway down the Napeague stretch of Route 27, between Amagansett and Montauk, at a place called the Lobster Roll, a famed fish shack "affectionately known as Lunch" (as the guidebooks say), serving up prototypical East End fare. In 1965, Fred Terry and his father, Richard, bought the Lobster Roll. With the help of Fred's mother, Sarah, his brother Dave, and his aunt Nellie, they turned a beach shanty into an area icon. Fred and Richard ran the restaurant, Sarah baked delicious homemade desserts, Dave shucked clams, and Nellie waited on tables. Twelve years later, Fred brought his then wife, Andrea, into the picture. Nearly three decades later, though most of the names have changed, the spirit of the Lobster Roll has remained very much the same—a warm, friendly, and casual restaurant, serving some of the best food on the East End to locals, tourists, and celebrities alike. Despite the countless write-ups and enormous success in this tony resort community, the Lobster Roll has maintained its down-to-earth feel.

Now run exclusively by Fred's ex-wife Andrea and general manager Paul DeAngelis (who after twenty years is truly a member of the family), the Lobster Roll has a loyal following that keeps the lines wrapped around the screened-in porch all season long. People come from great distances to sit on wooden benches and sink their teeth into the renowned lobster roll, a heavenly combination of succulent lobster meat subtly held together by mayonnaise and celery.

The Lobster Roll is the quintessential summer restaurant, and this book is the quintessential summer cookbook, filled with simple, mouthwatering recipes—classic dishes everyone likes to prepare (and eat) from Memorial Day through Labor Day. It's not a cookbook made up exclusively of recipes from the Lobster Roll (though it has many of these), but instead offers recipes that are universally associated with summer: grilled corn, juicy hamburgers, homemade lemonade, seafood chowder, shrimp salad, crab cakes, and of course the restaurant's namesake sandwich, all adapted for the home cook. We hope that by using the freshest ingredients at their peak season, you will be able to say, "It tastes *better* when it's made at

home." (These days the Lobster Roll feeds never-ending crowds, so we decided to bring in fruit pies from one of the wonderful local farm stands. But the pie recipes in this book are variations on the family recipes passed on by Sarah Terry.)

In addition to the restaurant's recipes and traditions, we have also included some family and area recipes: pickled zucchini with mint has been a Della Femina tradition for generations; Raspberry Peach Cobbler from Round Swamp Farm was graciously given to us by the Snyder-Niggles family; the Fresh Yellowfin Tuna Salad Sandwich is from East Hampton's Plain & Fancy; bloody marys and margaritas are from local bar-

tender Bob Barzilay; Grilled Soy-Ginger Swordfish Kabobs and Southsides are from friends Sue Devitt and Tim Bogardus; Lavender-and-Buttermilk Fried Chicken is from chef Rebecca Rubel; and the Stovetop Clambake is from Stuart's Seafood Market in Amagansett.

Welcome to summer in the Hamptons.

a note on ingredients

In many instances, the recipes throughout the book call for very specific ingredients: Hellmann's Mayonnaise, extra-virgin olive oil, superfine sugar, Sacramento Tomato Juice, Old Bay Seasoning, lime-wasabi mustard, and so forth. The key to a successful dish begins with the highest-quality ingredients; the whole is a sum of its parts.

For all of the recipes that call for salt, we prefer to use kosher salt for cooking, and a sprinkle of sea salt before serving. Table salt is a fine-grained refined salt with additives; kosher salt is an additive-free coarse-grain salt; and sea salt comes from the evaporation of sea water, and is generally large-grained and the costliest. Some argue that sea salt is the saltiest because of the large grains, while others believe the opposite. It's worth experimenting and finding your favorite for cooking and serving.

Try to buy all your fresh food—produce, meats, and fish—from a local purveyor who you've come to trust, and who specializes in that particular ingredient. Some tips to remember: Always look for whole fish that have clear eyes (cloudy eyes are a sign that the fish is not at its peak); fish fillets should never smell "fishy," and should always be resilient to the touch; produce needn't be picture perfect to taste its best, though sometimes it works out this way; softer peaches and small strawberries are almost always exponentially sweeter than their larger, firmer cousins. Most of us are extremely lucky to live in areas where we are able to forget that foods actually have a season, because so much is imported and available year-round. But try to buy according to the season in your area, and you will truly taste the difference.

Jodi Della Femina and Andrea Terry

appetizers and soups

Oysters on the Half Shell

Clams Casino

Steamers and Broth

Fried Calamari with Marinara Sauce

Bay Mussels in White Wine

Lobster Bisque

Manhattan Seafood Chowder

New England Clam Chowder

Cold Cucumber Soup

Chilled Carrot Soup

Gazpacho

oysters
on the half shell

PHOTOGRAPH ON PAGE 23

We find that oysters are easier to open if you chill them first for approximately 15 minutes, directly in the freezer or simply on ice.

24 oysters, rinsed and shucked (see Sidebar, page 22)
4 lemon wedges

Cocktail Sauce (recipe follows)
Mignonette Sauce (recipe follows)

Remoulade (recipe follows)
Tabasco sauce (optional)

Serve the oysters in a large bowl filled with crushed ice, lemon wedges, and ramekins of the sauces. Have a bottle of Tabasco sauce available for those who like an added kick.

oysters

We recommend trying different varieties and deciding for yourself which you prefer. Oysters grown in southern locations tend to be milder, while those grown in the north are a bit saltier, or "briny." When you put a raw bar together, we suggest mixing as many types as you can, such as:

Malpeque: Canadian—briny; Blue Point: Long Island—briny;

Welfleet: Massachusetts—briny; Kumamoto: Washington—pungent;

Chincoteague: Virginia—mild; Belón: France (also grown in Maine)—full flavored

Always choose oysters that are heavy to the touch and completely closed. Store them in a bowl inside the refrigerator with the rounded side of the oyster facing down in order to maintain their juices. Place a towel over the bowl, but do not keep them on ice—oysters should be iced no more than one hour before serving.

cocktail sauce

1 cup Heinz ketchup
1 lemon, juiced, to yield
   2 tablespoons fresh lemon
   juice

1 tablespoon prepared
   horseradish
½ teaspoon Worcestershire
   sauce

1 to 2 drops Tabasco sauce
   (optional)

In a medium bowl, combine all the ingredients. Refrigerate for 30 minutes before serving.

mignonette sauce

½ cup red wine vinegar
   (feel free to substitute
   champagne vinegar or
   flavored vinegar)

2 shallots, minced
1 tablespoon chopped fresh
   flat-leaf parsley

Salt and freshly ground
   black pepper, to taste

In a small bowl, whisk together the vinegar, shallots, and parsley. Season with salt and pepper and refrigerate until ready to serve.

remoulade

2 cups Hellmann's
   mayonnaise
3 tablespoons green sweet
   relish
2 garlic cloves, minced
2 teaspoons capers

1 tablespoon anchovy paste
1 teaspoon Dijon mustard
1 tablespoon fresh lemon
   juice (from about
   ½ lemon)

½ teaspoon Worcestershire
   sauce
Salt and freshly ground
   black pepper, to taste

In a medium bowl, combine all the ingredients. Refrigerate for several hours to allow the flavors to marry.

shucking oysters

Be sure to use only oysters that are firmly closed and well scrubbed. Using either a kitchen towel or, if available, an oyster glove, hold the oyster firmly. Gently slide the tip of the oyster knife into the "hinge" of the oyster (most often this is the narrowest part of the oyster, and is where the two shells meet), and carefully slide the knife around the shell so that you can loosen it without doing any damage to the oyster meat itself. Once you have access to the inside of the shell, use the knife on the underside of the top shell to loosen the oyster meat. Pry off the top shell, and loosen the meat from the bottom half, being careful not to lose any of the oyster juice.

OPPOSITE: Oysters on the Half Shell (recipe on pages 20-21). ABOVE AND RIGHT: Shucking an oyster, steps one and two.

clams casino

This is a great dish for those who want to eat clams on the half shell but get a little squeamish at the thought of ingesting a raw clam. Clams Casino is a delicious combination of cooked clam and crispy bacon served in a clam shell for a perfect summer appetizer.

2 garlic cloves, minced

¼ cup extra-virgin olive oil

¼ cup minced shallots (from about 2 shallots)

¼ cup minced green bell pepper (from about ⅓ cored and seeded pepper)

¼ cup minced red bell pepper (from about ⅓ cored and seeded pepper)

2 tablespoons white wine

2 tablespoons chopped fresh flat-leaf parsley

1 teaspoon dried oregano

½ teaspoon freshly ground black pepper

24 littleneck clams, shucked, meat separated from the shell, half the shells reserved

2 to 3 bacon strips, cut into 24 small pieces

4 lemons, cut in sixths

purchasing clams

Clams are sold by the size: littlenecks are the smallest, then top necks, cherrystones, and chowder clams. The larger the clam, the tougher the meat tends to be. We mostly use littleneck clams as they're the smallest and subsequently the most tender. Clam bellies (used to make our clam roll, page 52) are also known as soft-shell clams, belly clams, or steamers. Clam bellies are very easy to shuck since their shells do not close tightly. When purchasing soft-shell clams, be sure that they're alive (the neck should contract when touched); discard any dead clams or any with broken shells.

reheat the broiler.

In a medium saucepan, sauté the garlic in the olive oil over medium heat for about 2 minutes, until the garlic is transparent. Add the shallots and bell peppers, and cook for 3 to 5 minutes, until the peppers are tender. Add the wine, parsley, oregano, and black pepper, and simmer for about a minute longer. Remove the pan from the heat and pour the ingredients into a medium bowl.

Arrange the clam shells on a cookie sheet and spoon one piece of clam and the shallot-pepper mixture into each of 24 half shells; top with a piece of bacon. Broil the clams for 3 to 4 minutes, until sizzling and lightly browned. Serve immediately with the lemon wedges.

steamers and broth

Half the fun of steamers is the mere process of eating them—pulling the steamer from its shell, dipping it in warm water to remove any remaining sand, then dipping it in melted butter, and finally eating it as you pull the skin off the neck of the clam.

1 cup white vinegar
6 pounds live steamer clams

1 celery stalk, roughly
  chopped

¾ pound (3 sticks) salted
  butter

begin by cleaning the steamers in a large pot filled with the vinegar and ice-cold water to cover (see Note). Allow the steamers to soak for at least 30 minutes, then rinse in cold water and drain in a large colander.

Fill a tall, narrow pot with 2 inches of water and the celery and bring to a rapid boil. Carefully add the steamers to the pot, so that the shells don't break. Cover and cook over high heat for 8 minutes, or until the shells open; discard any that don't open. Meanwhile, melt the butter over low heat in a medium saucepan and divide among 6 small bowls.

Transfer the cooked steamers to medium serving bowls, discard the celery, and ladle the steamer broth (the water left in the pot) into separate small bowls. Serve immediately with the melted butter and more bowls for discarding the shells.

cleaning steamers

Fill a large pot with ice-cold water and 1 cup of white vinegar. Allow the steamers to soak in this mixture for at least 30 minutes before rinsing once again and draining in a colander. Vinegar is the secret to de-sanding steamers during the cleaning process. Live steamers dislike an acidic environment, and will naturally purge themselves of any excess sand.

steamer pots

Steamer pots are ideal for steaming all shellfish (mollusks and crustaceans). They are very large, and have a spigot built into the bottom half of the pot to pour off any broth; they also contain an inner basket that makes the cooking process even simpler. They are available at most hardware stores, seafood markets, and cooking-supply stores.

fried calamari with marinara sauce

The most important thing to remember when making fried calamari is not to overcook it or it will get too rubbery and taste more like pencil erasers than fish.

1½ cups all-purpose flour
2 tablespoons cornstarch
1 teaspoon dried oregano
1 teaspoon dried parsley
1 teaspoon onion powder
1 teaspoon garlic powder

1 teaspoon salt
½ teaspoon freshly ground white pepper
3 pounds squid, cleaned and cut into ½-inch rings

Peanut oil, for deep frying
2 cups Marinara Sauce (recipe follows), for dipping

In a medium bowl, combine the flour, cornstarch, oregano, parsley, onion and garlic powders, salt, and pepper. Dredge the calamari in the mixture.

Fill a large deep pot with 3 to 4 inches of peanut oil, and heat to 375°F. on a candy thermometer (or heat until a sprinkle of flour browns immediately when dropped in). Add the calamari in batches to avoid crowding the pan, and cook for 1½ minutes, or until golden brown. Remove with tongs or a slotted spoon, drain on paper towels, and serve hot with marinara sauce.

marinara sauce

MAKES ABOUT 4 CUPS

¼ cup extra-virgin olive oil
4 to 5 large garlic cloves,
  minced

1 28-ounce can whole
  tomatoes, in purée
½ cup loosely packed fresh
  basil, chopped

¼ cup red wine
1 teaspoon dry oregano
Salt and freshly ground
  black pepper, to taste

In a medium pot, heat the oil over a medium flame. Add the garlic and cook until golden but not brown, about 1 minute. Add the tomatoes, basil, wine, oregano, and salt and pepper. Break up the tomatoes with a wooden spoon and simmer over medium heat for 30 minutes, until the flavors marry and the sauce is a thick, chunky consistency.

SPECIALS

★ ★ ★ ★ ★ ★ ★ ★ ★

Broiled Combo Platter... 17⁵⁰
(Shrimp & Scallops)

Catch of the Day (Mahi-Mahi)... 16⁹⁵

Fisherman's Combo Platter... 17⁵⁰
(oysters & clam strips)

Coconut Shrimp & Chips... 16⁹⁵

Surf + Turf Platter... 18⁷⁵
(steak + stuffed shrimp)

BBQ Ribs Platter.... 17⁵⁰

Charbroiled Combo Platter 19⁹⁵
(Tuna + Sword)

Stuffed Flounder Platter.... 18⁵⁰

Savory Stuffed Shrimp ... 18⁵⁰

New York Stip Steak ... 17⁹⁵

North Atlantic Salmon .. 16⁹⁵

DUE TO

bay mussels in white wine

Be sure to serve this dish with crisp French bread (we love the fresh bread baked daily at Round Swamp Farm or Plain & Fancy in East Hampton) for dipping, and with spoons so that every last drop of broth can be enjoyed.

4 garlic cloves, minced
¼ cup shallots, minced
4 ounces (1 stick) salted butter
2 tablespoons extra-virgin olive oil

¼ cup scallions, finely chopped
1 cup dry white wine
2 tablespoons chopped fresh basil

2 tablespoons chopped fresh flat-leaf parsley
½ teaspoon dried oregano
Freshly ground black pepper, to taste
3 pounds mussels, rinsed

In a large pot, sauté the garlic and shallots in the butter and olive oil over medium heat for about 5 minutes, until the garlic and shallots are lightly browned. Add the scallions and cook for 1 more minute, then add the wine, basil, parsley, oregano, and pepper. Simmer for another minute, and add the mussels. Cover and simmer over medium heat for 7 to 8 minutes, until the mussels open, stirring halfway through. Discard any mussels that don't open.

lobster bisque

We like trying to find as many uses for the East End's local lobsters as possible. Though this bisque might seem time-consuming, it's well worth the effort. Perfect on a chilly, rainy summer day.

5 cups chicken stock or clam broth

3 1½-pound live male lobsters, rinsed in cold water

1 medium onion, peeled and chopped into 1-inch pieces

4 celery stalks, cut into 1-inch pieces

1 bay leaf

1 teaspoon dried thyme

½ cup plus 3 tablespoons loosely packed fresh flat-leaf parsley, roughly chopped

½ cup (1 stick) salted butter

½ cup all-purpose flour

2 cups whole milk

½ cup heavy cream

½ cup tomato purée

½ teaspoon paprika

¼ teaspoon freshly grated nutmeg

¼ teaspoon freshly ground white pepper

½ cup sherry

3 tablespoons chopped chives, for garnish

In a large pot, bring the stock or broth to a boil, and place the lobsters in the pot claws first. Cover and cook for 10 to 12 minutes, until the lobsters turn bright red. Halfway through the cooking, quickly remove the lid and turn the lobsters to ensure even cooking, then replace the lid immediately. Remove the lobsters, reserve the broth, and set the lobsters aside to cool. Measure 4 cups of the reserved broth, and return it to the pot. (If the broth measures less than 4 cups, add more chicken stock or clam broth.)

Remove the lobster meat from the claws, knuckles, and tails, chop fine, and set aside. Gather all of the lobster shells, wrap small batches of them in a clean towel, and use a mallet or the underside of a cleaver to crack the shells into smaller pieces. Then chop the body of the lobster into smaller pieces using a large chef's knife, and return with all of the shells to the lobster pot. Add the onion, celery, bay leaf, thyme, and ½ cup of the parsley, and simmer, covered, for 30 minutes.

Remove from the heat, and strain through a fine sieve, discarding the solids. You will need 3 cups of stock for the soup. Add more chicken stock or clam broth if necessary, and set aside.

In a large pot, melt the butter over low heat. Add the flour and whisk until well blended. Slowly add the reserved stock, whisking constantly. Reduce the heat to low and simmer.

Meanwhile, in a medium saucepan over a low flame, heat the milk, cream, and tomato purée until hot but not boiling. Pour the mixture into the stock, whisking continuously. Add the paprika, nutmeg, and pepper, and bring to a boil, still whisking. Reduce the heat to medium, add the sherry, and simmer for 5 to 7 minutes. Add the reserved lobster meat, mix well, and ladle the bisque into bowls. Garnish each bowl with the remaining parsley and the chives.

manhattan seafood chowder

We decided to change this recipe at the Lobster Roll and move from a traditional Manhattan clam chowder to this seafood chowder. We found that people loved the addition of the shrimp, cod, and scallops. Try adding okra and Tabasco to make this more of a seafood gumbo.

1 to 2 bacon strips
2 tablespoons extra-virgin olive oil
3 garlic cloves, minced
1 small onion, diced
1 celery stalk, diced
½ cup diced green bell pepper
1 carrot, peeled and diced
2 cups chopped canned tomatoes

1 tablespoon Worcestershire sauce
1 teaspoon dried thyme
1 teaspoon dried oregano
½ teaspoon Old Bay Seasoning
1 large potato, peeled and diced
8 cups clam broth
1 pound cod, cut into 1-inch pieces

1 pound small shrimp (sized 36 to 40 per pound), peeled, deveined, tails removed, and halved
1 pound sea scallops, halved
12 cherrystone clams, shucked and chopped
3 tablespoons chopped fresh flat-leaf parsley
Salt and freshly ground black pepper, to taste

heat a large pot over a medium flame. Add the bacon and cook until it renders 1 to 2 tablespoons of fat, about 5 minutes. Remove the bacon with a slotted spoon and discard. Add the olive oil and garlic to the rendered fat and cook for 30 seconds. Add the onion, celery, bell pepper, and carrot, and cook for 5 to 7 minutes, until lightly browned, stirring occasionally with a wooden spoon. Add the tomatoes, Worcestershire, thyme, oregano, and Old Bay Seasoning. Cook for another 2 to 3 minutes, stirring occasionally. Add the potato and clam broth, turn up the heat, and bring to a boil. Reduce the heat to low and simmer for 8 to 10 minutes, until the potatoes are tender.

Add the cod, shrimp, scallops, and clams. Mix well with a wooden spoon, stir in the chopped parsley, and season with salt and pepper. Cook for 5 minutes, until all the seafood is cooked through, and serve immediately.

new england clam chowder

Most recipes for classic New England clam chowder tend to be more brothy—we've experimented with many. This version served at the Lobster Roll is thick and creamy and full of flavor. Serve with oyster crackers or just plain saltines.

2 tablespoons salted butter
3 to 4 tablespoons
   all-purpose flour
2 bacon strips
2 tablespoons unsalted
   butter
4 medium garlic cloves,
   minced
1 small onion, diced

2 medium carrots, peeled
   and diced
6 tablespoons diced, cored,
   and seeded green bell
   pepper (about ½ pepper)
2 medium celery stalks,
   diced
3 medium potatoes, peeled
   and diced

4 cups clam broth
3 cups half-and-half
3 dozen chowder clams,
   shucked and chopped
2 tablespoons chopped fresh
   flat-leaf parsley
¼ teaspoon freshly ground
   white pepper
Salt (optional)

In a small sauté pan, make a roux by melting the salted butter. Add 3 tablespoons of the flour, whisking the mixture constantly until it pulls away from the sides of the pan. (More flour may be added if necessary.) Set aside.

Heat a 6-quart pot over a medium flame. Add the bacon and cook until it renders 1 to 2 tablespoons of fat, about 5 minutes. Remove the bacon with a slotted spoon, and discard. Add the unsalted butter and garlic to the rendered fat and cook for 30 seconds. Add the onion, carrots, bell pepper, and celery, and cook for 10 to 12 minutes, until the vegetables are slightly softened; do not overcook. Add the potatoes and broth, and simmer for 20 minutes, until the potatoes are tender. Stir in the half-and-half, bring to a boil, and reduce the heat to a simmer, stirring frequently.

In a medium bowl, combine 2 cups of liquid from the chowder pot with the reserved roux, whisk well, and return the mixture to the pot, stirring constantly until the soup thickens. Add the chopped clams, parsley, and freshly ground pepper (salt is optional, though the chowder probably won't need any). Cook 5 to 7 minutes, then serve with crackers.

NOTE: This creamy soup will thicken in the refrigerator, so feel free to whisk in a little extra milk when reheating to bring it back to the desired consistency.

cold cucumber soup

The secret ingredient here is East Hampton's Round Swamp Farm's homemade bread-and-butter pickles, which are unlike any others—sweet and savory at the same time. They add an unidentifiable special zing to this refreshing soup.

6 medium pickling cucumbers, peeled and roughly chopped, 8 thin slices reserved for garnish

1 cup Round Swamp Farm bread-and-butter pickles, with pickle juice and sliced onions (any sweet pickles may be substituted if necessary)

1½ cups heavy cream
1½ cups plain low-fat yogurt
4 ounces sour cream
Juice of 1 lemon
2 teaspoons salt
Snipped dill, for garnish

In a food processor or blender, purée the chopped cucumbers, the pickles and their juice, the heavy cream, yogurt, sour cream, lemon juice, and salt. Transfer to a medium bowl or container and refrigerate until well chilled. Garnish each bowl with 2 cucumber slices and a sprinkle of dill.

the lighter side

If you're looking for a light summer soup, but you don't want to lose the creamy texture, substitute plain low-fat yogurt for heavy cream. The soup will taste incredibly rich with a substantial drop in calories.

round swamp farm's bread-and-butter pickles

Round Swamp Farm (the Lester Farm) is a family-run farm that has been around for more than three hundred years. It is truly one of our favorite spots on the East End, and when Carolyn Lester and Harold Snyder open their doors each April, it is the first

sign that spring has truly begun, and summer is almost here. The bread-and-butter pickles have such a following that many customers stock up on these Mason jar–filled delicacies for the winter months when Round Swamp is closed. They're available through mail order (631-324-4438), and we can't recommend them enough for the cucumber soup.

chilled carrot soup

Though this recipe is for carrots, feel free to experiment a little. We sometimes alternate zucchini, or when we're feeling especially creative, we mix the two together and make a chilled carrot-and-zucchini soup.

1 bunch of scallions, rinsed and diced

1 to 2 tablespoons salted butter

3 pounds carrots, diced

5 cups chicken broth

2 bunches of watercress, cleaned

1 pint plain yogurt, for garnish

Minced chives, for garnish

In a large pot, sauté the scallions in 1 tablespoon of the butter for 2 minutes over medium heat. Add the carrots and continue to sauté for 3 minutes, adding more butter if necessary. Add the chicken broth, cover, and cook for 10 minutes, or until the carrots are tender. Add the watercress and cook for 3 minutes. Remove from the heat and let cool to room temperature. Once cool, purée either by using a hand blender or by processing the soup in batches in a food processor or blender. Refrigerate until ready to serve. Serve chilled with a dollop of yogurt and minced chives.

gazpacho

The secret to this gazpacho is adding mayonnaise, which lightens the color just a bit and adds a slightly creamy flavor to this piquant and refreshing soup. Depending on the size and strength of your blender, you may have to purée in batches.

2½ pounds (approximately 8) medium beefsteak tomatoes, stemmed and quartered

1 seedless cucumber, peeled, ends removed, and roughly chopped

1 orange bell pepper, seeded, stemmed, and roughly chopped

1 jalapeño pepper, seeded, stemmed, and roughly chopped

1 small red onion, roughly chopped

½ pound string beans, tips removed and roughly chopped

1 small bunch of chives, finely chopped

Juice of 1 lemon

3 cups tomato juice

¼ cup extra-virgin olive oil

1 teaspoon granulated sugar

1 tablespoon salt

1 teaspoon freshly ground black pepper

½ teaspoon cayenne pepper

3 tablespoons Hellmann's mayonnaise

In a food processor or blender, purée the tomatoes, cucumber, bell pepper, japapeño, onion, string beans, and chives and transfer to a medium bowl. Add the lemon juice, tomato juice, olive oil, sugar, salt, pepper, and cayenne and stir well to combine. Transfer back to the food processor or blender and add the mayonnaise. Mix once more, then transfer back to a bowl or container and refrigerate until well chilled.

rolls and sandwiches

Lobster Roll

Shrimp Salad

Fresh Yellowfin Tuna Salad Sandwich

Sautéed Soft-Shell Crab

Clam Roll

The Perfect Hamburger

lobster roll

PHOTOGRAPH ON PAGE 46

This sandwich is so flawless that it has a restaurant—and this book—named after it. The version here, adapted for home kitchens, starts with steamed whole lobsters, though at the Lobster Roll we buy fresh lobster meat. It takes so many lobsters to yield 2 pounds of lobster meat, and the process of steaming and cleaning is so labor-intensive, that we think the time you save by buying fresh lobster meat from your local seafood purveyor is well worth the added expense.

2 pounds freshly picked lobster meat, chilled and chopped into chunks, or 10 pounds live lobsters, steamed and meat removed (see Sidebar)

1 cup chopped celery (from 3 to 4 celery stalks), drained (see Note)
¾ to 1 cup Hellmann's mayonnaise
½ teaspoon salt

¼ teaspoon freshly ground black pepper
6 tablespoons (¾ stick) unsalted butter, softened
6 hot dog buns

In a medium bowl, combine the lobster meat, celery, and mayonnaise and gently toss until well mixed. Season with the salt and pepper and chill for at least 30 minutes (or up to overnight) before serving.

Preheat a large heavy skillet over medium flame. Lightly butter both sides of each bun and cook for 2 minutes per side, until golden brown. (The buns may also be toasted under a broiler.) When toasted, stuff them with the chilled lobster salad and serve immediately.

NOTE: When celery is chopped, it tends to release its natural moisture, which can water down the lobster salad and give it a soupy consistency. To avoid this, chop the celery, wrap it in a dry clean towel or several paper towels, and place in the refrigerator for 15 to 20 minutes, allowing the towel to absorb any excess moisture.

steaming lobsters and removing the meat

We recommend steaming lobsters instead of boiling them, as steaming is a slower cooking process and results in a more tender meat. Steaming is also more forgiving than boiling (there is less of a chance of overcooking), and since the water does not penetrate into the meat as it does when boiling, the meat is much more flavorful and succulent. When steaming, however, it is very important not to overcrowd the pot or the lobsters will not cook properly. A 5-gallon pot is ideal for steaming up to 8 pounds of lobster; for this recipe you will need to steam the lobsters in two batches. Fill the steamer pot with 1 inch of water and 1 tablespoon salt. Place the steaming rack inside the pot, cover, and bring the water to a rapid boil over high heat. As soon as the water boils, place the lobsters in the pot claws first and cover tightly. Turn the lobsters after 8 minutes to ensure even cooking. The lobster is done when the shell turns bright red, the tail meat is white without any translucency, and the lobster roe (if it has any) is also bright red. The total cooking time should be about 15 minutes per batch.

To remove the meat, allow the lobsters to cool completely, then break off the tail. Using a large knife, slice through the underside of the tail section. Remove and discard the tomalley and roe (if working with a female lobster). Crack the claws and knuckles (using lobster crackers) and remove the meat.

The green substance found in the carapace of the lobster is referred to as tomalley, or the liver and pancreas. As these organs accumulate environmental contaminants, many suggest that they should be discarded; some, though, claim it to be a delicacy.

LEFT AND OPPOSITE: Lobster Roll (recipe on page 44).

shrimp salad

We like to use small shrimp in this salad so that we can leave them whole—a bonus when it comes to salad presentation. If you wish to use slightly larger shrimp that can still remain intact, we recommend substituting a pound of 31–40 shrimp prepared in the same way.

1 teaspoon shrimp spice, in a mesh basket (see Note)
1½ pounds small shrimp (50–70 per pound), tails removed, peeled, and deveined
½ to ¾ cup Hellmann's mayonnaise

¾ cup chopped celery (from 2 stalks), drained (see Note, page 44)
1 tablespoon fresh lemon juice (from ½ lemon)
1 garlic clove, minced
½ teaspoon salt

2 tablespoons finely chopped onion (from ¼ onion)
¼ teaspoon freshly ground black pepper
3 tablespoons salted butter, softened
4 hot dog buns

bring 1 quart of water and the shrimp spice to a rapid boil. Add the shrimp and cook for 1 minute. Turn off the heat, stir and allow the shrimp to sit in the hot water for 3 to 4 minutes, or until fully cooked. Rinse, drain well, wrap in a clean, dry towel, and place in the refrigerator for several hours. (It is essential for the shrimp to be completely free of any excess moisture to avoid watering down your salad, and it's best to keep the shrimp cold during this drying.) In a medium bowl, combine the dry shrimp, mayonnaise, celery, lemon juice, garlic, salt, onion, and pepper. Mix thoroughly and refrigerate until ready to serve.

Butter the buns and place them on a grill or under a broiler until lightly toasted. Fill with cold shrimp salad, and serve.

shrimp spice

Shrimp spice—also known as shrimp boil, crab boil, fish boil, or pickling spice—is sold at most supermarkets and specialty stores. It is a mixture of mustard seeds, peppercorns, bay leaves, whole allspice, cloves, dried ginger, and chiles. We like to pour it in a mesh tea strainer and add it to the boiling water when making shrimp.

fresh yellowfin tuna salad sandwich

You know the summer season has arrived when David Bernier of Plain & Fancy, a specialty store in East Hampton, starts making his fresh yellowfin tuna salad. This is a terrific twist on the classic, which we like to serve on fresh rosemary bread, also made daily at Plain & Fancy.

1/4 cup honey
1 tablespoon toasted sesame oil
1/8 cup soy sauce
4 6-ounce yellowfin tuna steaks, each 2 inches thick

1/2 cup Hellmann's mayonnaise
1 tablespoon finely chopped red onion (from about 1/4 small onion)

1 tablespoon fresh lemon juice (from about 1/2 lemon)
Salt and freshly ground black pepper, to taste
8 thick slices of rosemary bread or country bread

Preheat a gas grill to medium-high or a charcoal grill until the embers are glowing.

In a small bowl, combine the honey, sesame oil, and soy sauce. Brush the mixture onto the tuna steaks, and grill for 5 to 7 minutes on each side. Remove the tuna from the grill and set aside to cool.

When cool, break it into chunks and place in a medium bowl. Add the mayonnaise, onion, lemon juice, and salt and pepper; stir gently to combine. Divide evenly among 4 to 6 thick slices rosemary bread, top with another slice, cut in half on the diagonal, and serve.

sautéed soft-shell crab

We always try to take advantage of the very short soft-shell-crab season and serve them for dinner, in sandwiches, and in as many ways as we can come up with, though this simple recipe is tough to beat.

8 to 10 soft-shell crabs, cleaned and trimmed (see Sidebar), dried
½ cup all-purpose flour
¾ teaspoon Old Bay Seasoning

1 teaspoon salt
¼ teaspoon freshly ground black pepper
½ cup extra-virgin olive oil
4 tablespoons (½ stick) salted butter, softened

6 soft rolls
1 to 1½ cups Remoulade (page 21)
1½ lemons, cut in wedges, for serving

Lay the crabs out on a sheet pan covered with paper towels. Using a sharp knife, make slits in the claws and main body. (Soft-shell crabs have a high water content and they tend to "pop" when they are being cooked. The tiny slits allow excess moisture to release.)

In a medium bowl, mix the flour, Old Bay, salt, and pepper. Dredge each crab in the flour mixture, coating both sides well.

In a large sauté pan, heat the olive oil and 1 tablespoon of the butter until the mixture begins to sizzle. Carefully place the crabs in the pan, and cook for 3 to 4 minutes on each side, until crispy and golden brown. You may have to do this in batches.

Meanwhile, spread the remaining butter on the challah and place the bread on a grill or under a broiler until lightly toasted. Spread the remoulade on the toast and top with the sautéed crabs. Serve with lemon wedges.

cleaning soft-shell crabs

Using poultry shears, snip off the face of the crab, located directly behind the eyes—this will also instantly kill the crab. Lift one side of the top of the shell and snip off the gills, then repeat on the other side. Flip the crab over, and snip off the flap (known as the apron) *on the bottom of the crab. Rinse and pat dry as thoroughly as possible—the less water, the less the crabs will splatter when cooking.*

clam roll

A great way to serve fried clams—delicious for a picnic on the beach.

5 pounds large steamers (clam bellies), de-sanded (see page 26), rinsed, and shucked

2 cups all-purpose unbleached flour

1 cup finely ground cornmeal

1 tablespoon Old Bay Seasoning

1 tablespoon salt

Peanut oil, for frying

4 buns

1 cup Tartar Sauce (recipe follows)

remove the necks of the steamers and discard. Rinse the bellies well and drain.

Meanwhile, in a medium bowl, combine the flour, cornmeal, Old Bay, and salt, and mix well.

Fill a medium pot with 4 to 5 inches of peanut oil and heat to 375°F. on a candy thermometer (or heat until a sprinkle of flour browns immediately when dropped in).

Dredge the bellies in the flour mixture, then place them in a wire strainer and shake off any excess flour. Gently place the bellies in the hot oil using a slotted spoon. Fry them in small batches for 2 to 3 minutes, or until golden brown. Drain on paper towels, and transfer to a cookie sheet in a warm oven (250°F. to 300°F.) until all the bellies are cooked.

Meanwhile, lightly toast the buns on a grill or in a broiler or toaster. Thinly spread the tartar sauce on each bun, top with fried clam bellies, and serve.

tartar sauce

1 cup Hellmann's mayonnaise

3 tablespoons sweet relish

1 teaspoon fresh lemon juice (from about ¼ lemon)

1 teaspoon Dijon mustard

Salt and freshly ground black pepper, to taste

In a medium bowl, whisk together all of the ingredients. Refrigerate until ready to use.

the perfect hamburger

This is a truly decadent twist on the traditional burger. A pat of butter in the center melts as the burger cooks, keeping it perfectly moist and wonderfully rich.

8 tablespoons (1 stick) salted butter, softened
1 small bunch of chives, minced

2½ pounds ground sirloin
Salt and freshly ground black pepper, to taste
Olive oil, for drizzling

6 brioche rolls, halved
1 large beefsteak tomato, sliced
1 Vidalia onion, sliced

In a small bowl, combine the butter and chives by mashing them together with a fork. Place the mixture on plastic wrap and roll into a log. Refrigerate for 1 hour, or until firm, then slice into 6 even disks.

Preheat a gas grill to medium-high or a charcoal grill until the embers are glowing.

Form 6 patties with the ground sirloin and push one butter disk inside the center of each patty. Sprinkle with salt and pepper and grill for 6 to 7 minutes per side for medium-rare. Transfer to a platter.

Drizzle olive oil on both halves of the rolls and lightly toast them on the grill. Assemble the burgers with the sliced tomato and Vidalia onion, and dress with your favorite condiments.

NOTE: In place of the chives, feel free to use another herb or crumbled blue cheese together with the butter.

entrées

Steamed Lobster

Stovetop Clambake

Cracked-Pepper Scallops

Grilled Shrimp

Old-Fashioned Crab Cakes

Baked Lemon Salmon with Lemon-Dill Sauce

Grilled Soy-Ginger Swordfish Kabobs

Lavender-and-Buttermik Fried Chicken

Grilled Citrus Chicken

Roasted Long Island Duckling with
Peach-Apricot Glaze

Grilled Pork Tenderloin with Spicy Peach Salsa

Sliced Rib-Eye Steak with Chive Butter and
Crumbled Blue Cheese

Filet Mignon with Horseradish Sauce

Grilled Leg of Lamb with Garlic and Rosemary

Barbecued Ribs with Classic Barbecue Sauce

steamed lobster

Serving steamed lobsters can truly turn an ordinary meal into an event. Your guests will enjoy the process of extracting the meat from the shell, the sumptuous taste of a juicy piece of fresh lobster meat dipped in melted butter, even the special utensils. We do suggest you dress for the occasion and wear a bib, as lobster fun tends to get a bit messy.

1 tablespoon salt	Six 1½- to 1¾-pound live lobsters (see Sidebar)	1 pound (4 sticks) salted butter (see Note)

fill a large, tall, narrow pot with 2 inches of water and the salt and bring to a rapid boil. Place the lobsters in the pot, claws facing down, and cover. Steam the lobsters for 8 minutes, then turn with tongs. (Be very careful when removing the lid; the steam is very hot. Work quickly and cover the pot again.) Continue cooking for another 7 to 10 minutes, until they have turned bright red; the tail meat should be white with no translucency and if the lobster has roe, it should be bright red.

Meanwhile, melt the butter (see Note) and divide into 6 small bowls. Transfer the cooked lobsters to plates and serve with melted butter, lobster crackers, and bowls to discard the shells.

NOTE: We prefer leaving the milk solids in the butter, because we find that this is what gives the melted butter its delicious flavor. If you prefer clarified butter, simply use a large spoon to skim off the white frothy milk solids on the surface of the melted butter.

buying lobsters

American lobsters, or large-clawed lobsters, are the most common lobsters eaten in the United States. These are often referred to as Maine lobsters and are known for their meaty claws. They are found from Newfoundland to South Carolina, though most of the catch comes from Maine and Massachusetts.

When purchasing lobsters, be sure to look for lively ones whose tails curl under when the lobsters are lifted. Be aware that listlessness is a sign of a lobster that's been in the tank too long.

lobster age and gender

Lobsters grow to 1 pound over the first 6 to 7 years of their life and then grow 1 pound every 2 to 3 years following. Like people, the male is generally narrower through the "tail" and has bigger claws while the female has a child-bearing "tail" and roe (loved by many but not all). Most recipes call for meat from the entire lobster, as the chewier tail meat and tender claw make a wonderful mix and variation of texture. With the exception of the roe, the meat from both male and female tastes exactly the same.

stovetop clambake

This recipe was given to us by Charlotte and Bruce Sasso, the owners of Stuart's Seafood Market in Amagansett. It's a terrific indoor alternative to a clambake on the beach, and one that can be prepared ahead of time. We recommend assembling all of the ingredients in the pot (with the exception of the liquid), refrigerating it until you're ready to begin cooking, then adding in the broth. In 30 minutes your clambake is ready to serve. We like to follow it with S'mores (page 120) whenever possible.

3 onions, peeled and quartered
8 garlic cloves, peeled and halved
4 1-pound lobsters

2 dozen Little Neck clams, cleaned (see page 26)
2 pounds mussels, scrubbed and debearded
16 small red-skinned potatoes, halved

4 ears fresh corn, husked and silked
1 pound kielbasa (optional)
1 pound (4 sticks) salted butter, melted, for dipping
Lemon wedges, for serving

In a large kettle, layer (from bottom to top) the onions, garlic, lobsters, clams, mussels, potatoes, corn, and kielbasa. Add 5 to 6 inches of water (or chicken stock) and cover. (It's fine to use a little extra water, but try not to use less or it will evaporate, causing the seafood to burn.) Place over high heat and cook for 30 to 35 minutes, or until the potatoes are tender. Serve with melted butter and lemon wedges.

cracked-pepper scallops

It's very important when searing the scallops to make sure that the pan is hot enough so that when the natural juices from the scallops mix with the heated olive oil, the scallops will still caramelize on both sides. For the same reason, be sure to dry the scallops as thoroughly as possible.

3 pounds sea scallops
1 teaspoon paprika
1 teaspoon cracked or
  coarsely ground black
  pepper

¼ teaspoon cayenne pepper
5 tablespoons chopped fresh
  flat-leaf parsley
1 teaspoon salt

¼ to ½ cup extra-virgin
  olive oil
Lemon wedges, for serving

rinse the scallops with cold water, drain, and pat dry as thoroughly as possible. Line a large cookie sheet with wax paper, and arrange the scallops close together. Combine the paprika, with the black and cayenne pepper in a small bowl, and stir to combine. Sprinkle the pepper mixture and 3 tablespoons of the parsley over the scallops, and sprinke with the salt.

In a large nonstick skillet, heat enough oil to cover the bottom of the pan. When the oil begins to smoke, reduce the heat to medium-high and add the scallops, seasoned-side down. Cook for 2 to 4 minutes on each side, until they turn a deep golden brown. Serve with lemon wedges, and garnish with the remaining chopped parsley.

a twist on herbs

For a creative garnish, try deep-frying herbs in olive oil and tossing them in sea salt. Sage leaves work particularly well because of their texture and substantial size. Try using a small tea strainer so that you can keep the herbs together while frying.

grilled shrimp

This is an extremely simple dish that requires so little prep time that you can relax with your guests, or even spend more time at the beach. It also makes a great appetizer: just cut the recipe in half, or simply make more skewers with fewer shrimp on each.

5 to 6 large garlic cloves, minced

1 cup extra-virgin olive oil

¼ cup fresh lemon juice (from about 2 to 3 lemons)

2 tablespoons chopped fresh flat-leaf parsley

1 teaspoon salt

½ teaspoon freshly ground black pepper

Nonstick cooking spray

36 jumbo (sized 16–20 per pound) shrimp, peeled and deveined, tails intact

1 lemon, cut into 6 wedges, for garnish

In a medium bowl, combine the garlic, oil, lemon juice, parsley, salt, and pepper. Mix well and set aside. Spray stainless-steel or wooden skewers with nonstick cooking spray so the shrimp will slide off easily once cooked. Rinse the shrimp and pat dry. Place 6 shrimp on each skewer, and place the skewers in a large (preferably oblong) baking dish. Using a pastry brush, thoroughly cover the shrimp with the marinade, and refrigerate for 20 minutes.

Preheat a gas grill to medium or a charcoal grill until the embers glow.

Place the skewered shrimp on the grill and cook for 2 to 4 minutes on each side, basting frequently with the marinade, until they are firm to the touch and the inside turns opaque. Serve with lemon wedges.

NOTE: To keep wooden skewers from burning be sure to presoak them for at least 1 hour.

cleaning shrimp

To peel or remove the shell from a shrimp, first remove the "legs" along with the rest of the shell. To devein, use a sharp knife to cut a ¼-inch slice along the back of the shrimp. Rinse out the vein under cold running water.

old-fashioned crab cakes

These crab cakes are bursting with flavor. We like to serve them as an entrée with remoulade and homemade coleslaw, or by themselves as an appetizer to a light seafood entrée.

4 large garlic cloves, minced
6 tablespoons extra-virgin olive oil
¼ cup finely chopped onion (about ½ medium onion)
⅓ cup finely chopped scallions
½ cup finely chopped celery (from 1 to 2 stalks)
2 tablespoons finely chopped green bell pepper (from about ¼ pepper)

2 tablespoons finely chopped red bell pepper (from about ¼ pepper)
2 tablespoons white wine
1 pound jumbo lump crabmeat, picked over for shells, drained, and squeezed dry
½ cup seasoned bread crumbs
½ cup grated Parmesan
2 tablespoons fresh lemon juice (from about 1 lemon)

2 jumbo eggs, lightly beaten
2 tablespoons chopped fresh flat-leaf parsley
2 teaspoons Dijon mustard
1 teaspoon Old Bay Seasoning
½ teaspoon salt
¼ teaspoon freshly ground black pepper
1 lemon, cut into 6 wedges, for garnish
2 cups Remoulade (page 21)

In a medium skillet over medium heat, cook the garlic in 3 tablespoons of the olive oil for about 3 minutes, until lightly browned. Add the onion, scallions, celery, and green and red peppers, and cook for about 5 minutes, until lightly browned. Add the wine, simmer for 1 minute, and remove from the heat. Transfer the mixture to a large bowl. Add the crabmeat and mix well. Add the bread crumbs, Parmesan, lemon juice, eggs, parsley, mustard, Old Bay, salt, and pepper, and mix until well blended. Line a cookie sheet with wax paper. Divide the crab mixture into 6 patties, place on the cookie sheet, and refrigerate for 1 hour.

In a large skillet, heat the remaining 3 tablespoons of oil and sauté the crab cakes for 3 to 4 minutes on each side, until fully cooked and lightly browned. Add more oil as needed. Serve immediately with lemon wedges and remoulade.

baked lemon salmon with lemon-dill sauce

This light summer dish is wonderful served either hot or cold, for lunch or dinner. It's a variation on a recipe given to us by fitness guru Radu Teodorescu, who likes to add tomatoes and peppers when baking; we prefer the simple flavors of the Lemon-Dill Sauce.

Extra-virgin olive oil for
   drizzling
3 lemons, washed and thinly
   sliced

2 pounds salmon fillet
1 teaspoon salt
1 teaspoon freshly ground
   black pepper

1¼ cups Lemon-Dill Sauce
   (recipe follows)

Preheat the oven to 450°F. Lightly grease a baking dish with olive oil.

Place two-thirds of the lemon slices in the greased baking dish. Place the salmon fillet on top of the bed of lemons, cover it with the remaining slices, drizzle with olive oil, and sprinkle with the salt and pepper. Bake for 20 to 25 minutes, until the salmon is a light pink on the outside and a deeper pink inside. Remove from the oven and either serve immediately or refrigerate until cool. Serve with the lemon-dill sauce.

lemon-dill sauce

MAKES ABOUT 1¼ CUPS

½ cup heavy cream
¼ cup sour cream

3 tablespoons fresh lemon
   juice (from about
   1½ lemons)

3 tablespoons fresh dill
Salt and freshly ground
   black pepper, to taste

In a food processor or blender, beat the heavy cream and sour cream until thick. Add the lemon juice, dill, salt, and pepper and blend until combined. Refrigerate until ready to serve.

grilled soy-ginger swordfish kabobs

We first tried these at our friend Sue Devitt's dinner party in Sag Harbor. They're simple to prepare, and they make for a light and fun meal with friends. We like to serve them the way we first had them—with homemade focaccia from Espresso's Italian Market in Sag Harbor (warm it slightly and watch everyone clamor for it!) and with Grilled Corn with Lime Juice (page 94).

2 pounds swordfish, cleaned, skin removed, and cut into 1- to 2-inch cubes
12 to 18 grape tomatoes
1 orange bell pepper, cored, seeded, and cut into 6 pieces

1 yellow bell pepper, cored, seeded, and cut into 6 pieces
1 small Vidalia onion, quartered and separated into individual layers
10 to 12 button mushrooms, stemmed and cleaned

1 lime, cut into 6 wedges
¾ cup teriyaki sauce
3-inch piece of peeled fresh ginger, grated
1 tablespoon sesame oil
2 garlic cloves, minced
Juice of 2 limes

Prepare the skewers by alternating the swordfish pieces, tomatoes, orange and yellow peppers, onion, mushrooms, and lime wedges. Place the skewers on a dish or platter or in a resealable plastic bag.

Prepare the marinade by mixing the teriyaki sauce, ginger, sesame oil, and garlic in a small bowl. Pour over the skewers and refrigerate for at least 2 hours, or as long as overnight.

Preheat a gas grill to medium-high or a charcoal grill until the embers are glowing. Squeeze the lime juice over the skewers and transfer them to the grill, brushing them liberally with the remaining marinade. Grill for 7 to 10 minutes per side, until the vegetables are browned and the swordfish is cooked through but still moist. Remove from the heat and serve.

lavender-and-buttermilk fried chicken

This is one of the best fried chicken recipes ever, passed on by chef Rebecca Rubel. The addition of lavender, an aromatic plant in the mint family, is the perfect touch to keep guests guessing—and coming back for more!

6 split chicken breasts on the rib bones with skin, or 3 whole breasts split in half
2 teaspoons kosher salt
2 teaspoons freshly ground black pepper

2 cups buttermilk
Canola or peanut oil, for deep-frying
2 cups all-purpose flour
1 teaspoon paprika
Pinch of cayenne pepper

1 teaspoon dried thyme
2 tablespoons dried lavender flowers
2 large eggs
1 cup whole milk

Rub the chicken breasts with 1 teaspoon of the salt and 1 teaspoon of the pepper, place in a nonreactive bowl or container, and cover with the buttermilk. Let marinate in the refrigerator for 12 hours or overnight.

Fill a heavy-duty or cast-iron pot (suitable for frying and large enough to hold all of the chicken) with 4 to 5 inches of oil, and heat to 350°F. on a candy thermometer (or heat until a sprinkle of flour browns immediately when dropped in). In a large bowl, combine the flour, paprika, cayenne, thyme, lavender, and remaining salt and pepper. In a separate bowl, make an egg batter by whisking together the eggs, milk, and 1 cup of water until smooth. Remove the chicken from the marinade and shake off any extra buttermilk clinging to the breasts. Working with one piece at a time, dredge the chicken in the flour mixture to coat, then dip into the egg batter, then dredge it once again in the flour mixture.

Carefully place the coated chicken one piece at a time into the hot oil; keep the thermometer in the oil and try to maintain the tempera-ture. Once you've placed all of the chicken in the oil, fry uncovered for 10 minutes, then flip the pieces over and fry for 10 minutes more, or until golden brown and crispy. Remove from the oil and drain on paper towels. Serve immediately.

grilled citrus chicken

Perfect for a hot and humid summer night, this light grilled chicken has lots of fresh flavor, a zesty alternative to the typically saucy barbecued fare.

2 cups orange juice
2 navel oranges, 1 zested
   and sliced, the other sliced
12 fresh basil leaves, washed
   and finely chopped

1 tablespoon salt
1 tablespoon honey
4 boneless chicken breast
   halves (2 pounds),
   washed and pounded

2 tablespoons (¼ stick)
   salted butter
1 tablespoon granulated
   sugar

In a bowl or container deep enough to marinate, combine the orange juice, orange zest, basil, salt, and honey and stir well to combine. Add the chicken and the slices of the zested orange and refrigerate for at least 2 hours and up to overnight.

Preheat a gas grill to medium or a charcoal grill until the embers are glowing. Transfer the chicken to the grill, brush liberally with the marinade (discard any remaining marinade and the orange slices), and cook for 10 to 12 minutes per side, until cooked through but still moist. Meanwhile, melt the butter in a medium sauté pan and add the remaining sliced orange and the sugar. Lightly sauté for 3 to 5 minutes, until the butter is absorbed and the oranges are warm. Remove the chicken from the grill and transfer to a serving platter garnished with the warm orange slices.

roasted long island duckling with peach-apricot glaze

A sweet twist on duck. Though this takes a while to roast, the actual preparation takes only a few minutes, and the end result is one that will truly impress your guests.

1 5½-pound Long Island duckling, rinsed	1 small bunch of fresh mint	3 tablespoons honey
1 navel orange, quartered	1 cup orange juice	1 cup dry white wine
	4 cups peach nectar	1 cup dried apricots

Preheat the oven to 375°F.

Place the duck on a roasting rack in a roasting pan, and stuff the cavity with the orange and mint. Pour the orange juice and 2 cups of the peach nectar over the duck, drizzle the honey on top of the skin, and place in the preheated oven. Bake for 1 hour and 45 minutes for medium rare, or longer if you prefer your duck more well done, flipping once after approximately 1 hour. The skin should be well browned on both sides before you remove the duck from the oven.

Meanwhile, in a medium saucepan, bring the remaining 2 cups of peach nectar, the white wine, and the dried apricots to a boil. Reduce the heat to low and simmer until the sauce is reduced and very thick, approximately 45 minutes.

Remove the duck from the oven, and let cool for 10 to 15 minutes. Transfer to a serving platter, and brush on the peach-apricot glaze. Serve immediately.

grilled pork tenderloin with spicy peach salsa

This dish is a wonderful combination of flavors; we love the smoky taste of the grilled pork mixed with the sweetness of fresh summer peaches and finished with the zing of spicy jalapeños.

2 jalapeño peppers, rinsed, seeded, and stemmed
6 tablespoons rice vinegar
8 teaspoons sugar
2 teaspoons salt, plus more to taste

4 large peaches, pitted and cubed into 1-inch pieces
2 tablespoons lime juice (from 1 to 2 limes)
4 tablespoons chopped fresh mint
3 tablespoons olive oil

¼ teaspoon cayenne pepper
½ teaspoon freshly ground black pepper
3 pork tenderloins (12 ounces each), each sliced into 6 medallions

In a blender or food processor, coarsely purée the jalapeños with ½ cup water. Transfer to a small saucepan, and add the vinegar, sugar, and 1 teaspoon of the salt. Stir to combine and cook over medium heat for 3 to 5 minutes, until the sugar has completely dissolved.

Remove from the heat and cool to room temperature. Transfer to a medium bowl and add the peaches, lime juice, and mint. Stir to combine, cover, and keep at room temperature for at least 30 minutes before serving.

Preheat a gas grill to medium or a charcoal grill until the embers are glowing.

In a small bowl, combine the oil, cayenne, the remaining teaspoon of salt, and the ½ teaspoon pepper. Massage the mixture evenly onto all sides of the pork medallions. Place on the grill and cook for 2 to 3 minutes per side, until cooked through. Remove from the grill and serve with the salsa.

sliced rib-eye steak with chive butter and crumbled blue cheese

This is always a crowd pleaser among meat lovers—but it's probably best not to mention all the olive oil, butter, and cheese until after the meal has been fully enjoyed.

3 tablespoons extra-virgin
   olive oil
1 teaspoon salt
1 teaspoon freshly ground
   black pepper

3 1-pound rib-eye steaks
   (1 inch thick), boned, at
   room temperature
6 tablespoons (¾ stick)
   salted butter, softened

2 tablespoons minced fresh
   chives
1½ cups crumbled blue
   cheese, preferably
   Gorgonzola

Preheat a gas grill to medium-high or a charcoal grill until the embers are glowing.

In a small bowl, combine the olive oil, salt, and pepper, and massage it evenly onto both sides of the steaks. Place the steaks on the grill and cook for 7 to 8 minutes per side, turning once, for a rare steak. Meanwhile, use a fork to mash the butter and chives together on a large serving platter, and spread the mixture evenly down the center. Once the steaks are done, remove from the grill, let rest for 5 minutes, then slice and arrange on top of the chive butter. Distribute the crumbled blue cheese evenly across the top, and serve.

filet mignon
with horseradish sauce

We always try to make extra filet so that we can use the leftovers to make Steak Salad (page 88) or sandwiches on fresh Tuscan bread the following day.

3 garlic cloves, crushed
2 teaspoons salt, plus more
    to taste
1 teaspoon freshly ground
    black pepper, plus more
    to taste

¼ cup extra-virgin olive oil
3 pounds beef filet, trimmed
    and tied by the butcher, at
    room temperature
⅛ cup fresh white
    horseradish, grated

⅛ cup heavy cream
½ cup sour cream
1 tablespoon fresh lemon
    juice (from about
    ½ lemon)

Preheat the oven to 350°F.

In a small bowl, combine the garlic, 2 teaspoons salt, 1 teaspoon pepper, and olive oil. Place the filet on a rack in a roasting pan and massage the oil mixture into the meat. Place it in the oven and bake for 30 minutes for "black and blue" (our preference), or 45 to 50 minutes for medium-rare.

Meanwhile, combine the horseradish, heavy cream, sour cream, lemon juice, and salt and pepper to taste in a bowl. Mix well and refrigerate until ready to use.

Remove the filet from the oven, let rest for 10 minutes, slice, and serve with the horseradish sauce.

grilled leg of lamb with garlic and rosemary

The key to this dish is in the cut: Butterflying the lamb makes the meat much easier to handle and grill, and removes much of the fat as it cooks, making it an almost healthy summer meal.

¾ cup extra-virgin olive oil
¼ cup red wine
4 garlic cloves, minced
3 tablespoons minced fresh
   rosemary leaves

1 tablespoon salt
1 tablespoon freshly ground
   black pepper

5- to 6-pound boneless and
   butterflied leg of lamb,
   trimmed of excess fat

In a medium bowl, combine the oil, wine, garlic, rosemary, salt, and pepper and whisk until well blended. Place the lamb on a large shallow platter and pour half of the marinade over the lamb; spread evenly using a pastry brush. Turn the lamb and pour the remaining marinade over the top and spread evenly once again. Cover with plastic wrap and let marinate in the refrigerator for at least 3 hours.

Preheat a gas grill to medium or a charcoal grill until the embers are glowing. Remove the lamb from the marinade, transferring the excess marinade to a small pan. Bring the excess marinade to a boil over medium heat, then set aside. Grill the lamb for 10 to 15 minutes on each side, or until an internal thermometer reads 160°F. for medium to medium-rare, basting with the marinade regularly. Once cooked, remove from the grill and allow to rest for 5 to 10 minutes. Slice and serve with the reserved marinade.

75

barbecued ribs with classic barbecue sauce

The quintessential food for a summer barbecue. It seems that no matter how many extra ribs we make, there are still never any left over. Though ribs do take quite a while to grill, and require some basting attention to keep them moist, they are truly worth the wait. We like to serve them with a classic barbecue sauce and buttery corn on the cob (see page 96).

2 tablespoons brown sugar
1 tablespoon paprika
1 tablespoon kosher salt
1 teaspoon freshly ground
  black pepper

½ teaspoon cayenne pepper
3 garlic cloves, minced
2 racks baby back pork or
  beef ribs (about 4 to
  5 pounds)

1 to 2 12-ounce cans of beer
1 batch Barbecue Sauce
  (recipe follows)

In a small bowl, combine the brown sugar, paprika, salt, peppers, and garlic. Massage the mixture over the ribs, wrap in aluminum foil, and refrigerate for 4 to 8 hours.

Preheat a gas grill to medium and set it up for indirect grilling by lighting the front and back burners. If you're using a charcoal grill, preheat the coals to medium, and then rake them into two piles on either side of the grill.

Pour the beer into a spray bottle. Spray the ribs liberally with the beer, and place them on the grill away from the heat, meaty-side up. Cover and cook for 30 to 40 minutes, spraying every 15 minutes with the beer. Turn the ribs and cook for 35 to 45 minutes longer, continuing to spray frequently. Brush both sides of the ribs with barbecue sauce, place them directly over the fire, and grill until brown, about 2 to 3 minutes per side.

Serve with additional sauce on the side.

barbecue sauce

MAKES ABOUT 1½ CUPS

1 cup ketchup
½ cup brown sugar
1 tablespoon honey
1 tablespoon molasses

1 tablespoon Worcestershire
  sauce
1 teaspoon paprika
1 teaspoon dry mustard

½ teaspoon freshly ground
  pepper
½ teaspoon cayenne pepper

In a small saucepan, combine all the ingredients and bring to a boil. Lower the heat and simmer for 4 to 6 minutes, stirring throughout, until thickened. Cool to room temperature and refrigerate until ready to use.

vegetables, sides,
and salads

simple caesar salad

A true Caesar salad is made with raw egg, an ingredient many feel apprehensive about using. For a safer alternative, try either coddling the egg (by gently boiling it for 2 minutes) to kill any bacteria, or buy pasteurized liquid eggs at your local market, a product that mixes the whites and yolks, then pasteurizes them in order to kill any bacteria without actually cooking the eggs.

1 head of romaine, thoroughly washed, dried, and chopped
2 cups croutons
1 large egg
4 ounces grated Parmesan cheese
2 garlic cloves

1 teaspoon salt
4 anchovy fillets
1/4 teaspoon freshly ground black pepper
1/8 teaspoon sugar
1/2 teaspoon Worcestershire sauce

1 teaspoon fresh lemon juice (from about 1/4 lemon)
1/4 teaspoon Dijon mustard
2 tablespoons red wine vinegar
1/2 cup extra-virgin olive oil

toss the romaine in a large salad bowl with the croutons, egg, and grated Parmesan.

On a flat plate, mash the garlic and salt together with a fork until combined. On the same plate (push the garlic mixture off to one side) finely chop the anchovies, and combine with the garlic mixture. Transfer to a jar with a lid, then add the pepper, sugar, Worcestershire, lemon juice, mustard, and vinegar. Cover and shake well. Add the olive oil, shake again until combined, then pour over the salad. Toss well and serve.

pickled squash and mint salad

One of my best childhood summer memories of my grandparents' house is sitting around a table in their backyard eating this salad. When the mint is full of flavor, and the squash has been absorbing the garlic and vinegar for hours, it's a taste that keeps you going back for seconds and thirds.

¾ to 1 cup extra-virgin olive oil

3 pounds (approximately 6) zucchini, washed and sliced with tips removed

6 garlic cloves, quartered

2 teaspoons salt

1 teaspoon freshly ground black pepper

½ to ¾ cup balsamic or red wine vinegar

1 bunch of fresh mint

heat ¼ cup of the oil in a large sauté pan until very hot. Add the zucchini in small batches and sauté, turning quickly with a fork, and removing before the zucchini gets too mushy, about 5 minutes. Transfer to a bowl without draining. Add more olive oil to the pan as needed, but be sure to give it time to get hot before adding more zucchini.

In a large bowl, layer the sautéed zucchini with the garlic, salt, pepper, vinegar, and mint. Refrigerate for 4 to 6 hours (the longer it stays in the refrigerator, the better it will taste). Bring to room temperature, lightly toss, and serve.

arugula salad with prosciutto and figs

Incredibly simple, colorful, and completely irresistible—this will impress your guests while taking only moments to pull together. The key is to use only the highest quality ingredients, especially the prosciutto, cheese, oil, and vinegar. The perfect last-minute opener to any summer meal.

2 bunches of arugula, washed and trimmed
8 to 10 slices of best-quality prosciutto

8 to 10 purple or green figs, rinsed, stemmed, and quartered
¼ pound Parmigiano-Reggiano (not grated), for shaving

¼ cup olive oil, for drizzling
¼ cup fig balsamic or balsamic vinegar, for drizzling

Spread the arugula on a large serving platter. Cover the greens with the sliced prosciutto, distribute the figs, and add a generous portion of shaved Parmigiano-Reggiano—enough to cover the whole salad. Drizzle the olive oil and balsamic vinegar, and serve.

tomato, vidalia onion, and basil salad

A simple and delicious salad that uses some of the best ingredients of the summer: juicy ripe tomatoes bursting with flavor, crunchy onion with a spicy but sweet taste, and fresh basil, so aromatic it infuses the whole kitchen with the scent of the season.

6 vine-ripened tomatoes, cut into wedges

1 medium Vidalia onion, coarsely chopped

2 cups loosely packed fresh basil leaves, chopped

¼ cup extra-virgin olive oil

2 tablespoons balsamic vinegar

Salt and freshly ground black pepper, to taste

In a medium bowl, combine the tomatoes, onion, and basil and set aside. In a small bowl, combine the olive oil and vinegar, and whisk until blended. Pour over the tomato mixture, season with salt and pepper, and toss well. Refrigerate and chill until ready to serve.

tomato and avocado with truffle oil

When the tomatoes and avocados are perfectly ripe, and the truffle oil has a chance to really do its thing, this simple salad becomes a true delicacy.

3 vine-ripened or 2 beefsteak tomatoes, cut into cubes
2 avocados, peeled, pitted, and cubed
1/8 cup extra-virgin olive oil
2 tablespoons white truffle oil
1/2 teaspoon salt
1/4 teaspoon freshly ground black pepper
1 tablespoon fresh lemon juice (from about 1/2 lemon)

toss the tomatoes, avocados, olive oil, truffle oil, salt, pepper, and lemon juice together in a large bowl. Let sit for at least 20 to 30 minutes at room temperature so the truffle oil flavor infuses properly.

roasted beet salad

Serve chilled or at room temperature. The beautiful red color of this often-overlooked root vegetable will brighten any table—and it's full of flavor.

16 fresh beets, peeled and
sliced ¼ inch thick
½ cup extra-virgin olive oil
4 garlic cloves, minced

2 tablespoons chopped fresh
oregano leaves or
1 tablespoon dried

½ teaspoon salt
¼ teaspoon coarsely ground
black pepper

Preheat the oven to 400°F.

Toss the beets with the olive oil and garlic until the beets are well coated. Place in a 13 × 9-inch baking dish and roast for 35 to 45 minutes, until tender, tossing throughout. Remove from the oven and transfer to a bowl. Toss well with the spices, and serve.

NOTE: To grill, blanch the beets for 7 to 10 minutes, then toss them in the oil, garlic, oregano, salt, and pepper. Finish on the grill for 30 seconds per side, until just seared.

handling beets

The rich, scarlet color of beets will add color to any summer plate. But to avoid adding the color to your hands and clothes, we recommend that you wear latex gloves and an apron throughout the cleaning and handling process—and be very, very careful.

steak salad

The key to making this salad taste great is using the juice from the meat in the dressing. Everyone we've served it to at lunches by the beach thinks it's a winner. We like to use wasabi-lime mustard, available at many specialty stores. If you have trouble finding it, a substitution of your favorite spicy mustard combined with a squeeze of fresh lime juice will work well too.

6 to 8 cups mesclun greens, washed and dried
1 red onion, chopped into ¼-inch dice
4 scallions, finely chopped
1 cup grape tomatoes

2 avocados, peeled, pitted, and cut into ½-inch cubes
One 1-pound rib-eye steak, grilled rare and thinly sliced (reserve the juices when cutting the meat)
½ cup vegetable oil

Dash of extra-virgin olive oil
¼ cup white wine vinegar
1 garlic clove, minced
1 teaspoon wasabi-lime mustard
2 teaspoons salt

In a large salad bowl, combine the greens, onion, scallions, tomatoes, avocados, and sliced steak, and toss to combine. In a small bowl, using a whisk, combine the reserved steak juices, oils, vinegar, garlic, mustard, and salt. Dress the salad, toss once more, and serve.

chopped tarragon and blue cheese salad

This is one of our favorite salads. Though there are many ingredients, it's extremely easy to prepare, and the mix of flavors is incredible—we try to include everything in each forkful. There's something so satisfying about a tart cranberry meeting a sweet grape, a crunchy walnut, some pungent blue cheese, and savory chives together in one bite. Some may call it overkill, but we think it's pure heaven.

½ head of iceberg lettuce, washed and chopped
2 endives, chopped
1 cup green grapes
1 pint sweet grape tomatoes
1 cup chopped walnuts
1 cup dried cranberries
1 avocado, peeled, pitted, and cubed

1 cucumber, sliced
½ pound crumbled blue cheese
1 bunch of chives, chopped
1 bunch of tarragon, chopped
3 tablespoons fresh lemon juice (from about 1 lemon)

2 tablespoons Dijon mustard
1 tablespoon Hellmann's mayonnaise
¼ teaspoon salt
⅛ teaspoon freshly ground black pepper
⅛ teaspoon Worcestershire sauce
½ cup extra-virgin olive oil

In a large salad bowl, combine the lettuce, endives, grapes, tomatoes, walnuts, cranberries, avocado, cucumber, blue cheese, chives, and tarragon.

For the dressing, in a food processor or blender, combine the lemon juice, mustard, mayonnaise, salt, pepper, and Worcestershire. Process on a low speed, and slowly add the olive oil until emulsified. Pour over the salad, toss well, and serve.

chopping herbs

A simple shortcut to chopping fresh herbs is to do away with your paring knife, and grab a scissors. Snipping chives, parsley, and the lot is a great way to speed up preparation, tossing, and garnishing.

macaroni salad

Ideal for a picnic or barbecue. You can turn this side salad into more of a meal by adding tuna or strips of grilled chicken, and serving it with a bowl of chilled soup as a light summer lunch. We sometimes add hard-boiled egg for a twist.

1 tablespoon plus
1 teaspoon kosher salt
1 pound elbow macaroni
1 cup chopped celery (from 2 to 3 stalks)
½ cup chopped onion (from about ½ onion)

½ cup chopped red bell pepper (from about ⅓ pepper)
¼ cup chopped green bell pepper (from about ¼ pepper)

¼ cup chopped scallions (about 2 scallions)
1½ cups Hellmann's mayonnaise
1 teaspoon Dijon mustard
½ teaspoon freshly ground black pepper

In a large pot, bring water and 1 tablespoon of the salt to a boil. Add the macaroni and cook for 7 to 8 minutes; drain, rinse with cold water, and drain again. Transfer to a large bowl and combine with the celery, onion, red and green peppers, scallions, and mayonnaise. Toss until well blended, then add the mustard, pepper, and remaining 1 teaspoon of salt. Mix well and chill in the refrigerator for several hours before serving.

roasted potatoes with chives

A great side dish to grilled steak or chicken. We personally love the flavor of chives, but you can easily change and enhance this dish by substituting rosemary, tarragon, marjoram, oregano, or nearly any favorite savory herb.

2½ pounds (approximately 5) large red potatoes, scrubbed and thinly sliced

¼ to ½ cup extra-virgin olive oil

1 bunch of chives, chopped

1 tablespoon kosher salt

1 teaspoon freshly ground black pepper

Preheat the oven to 450°F.

In a large bowl, toss the potatoes with the olive oil, chives, salt, and pepper. Spread them evenly over two cookie sheets and drizzle any remaining oil over the top. Roast the potatoes for approximately 30 minutes, rotating the pans every 7 to 10 minutes, until the potatoes are golden brown.

new potato salad with egg, onions, and peppers

An alternative to the simpler version made with only mayonnaise, salt, and pepper, this more complex salad combines the flavors and textures of peppers, onions, fresh dill, and hard-boiled egg. Great to serve with lunch or an evening barbecue or clambake.

2 teaspoons kosher salt

1½ pounds small red-skinned potatoes, cut into ½-inch chunks

1 medium Vidalia onion, coarsely chopped

¼ cup chopped green bell pepper (about ¼ pepper)

4 hard-boiled jumbo eggs, peeled and chopped (see Sidebar)

1 teaspoon Dijon mustard

1 cup Hellmann's mayonnaise

1 tablespoon chopped fresh dill

¾ teaspoon freshly ground black pepper

fill a large pot with water and 1 teaspoon of the salt, and bring the water to a rapid boil. Add the potatoes, reduce the heat to medium, and simmer until the potatoes are tender, approximately 15 to 20 minutes; do not overcook or the potatoes will become mushy. Remove from the heat, immediately drain, and rinse with cold water to halt the cooking process. Drain again.

While the potatoes are still hot, transfer to a large bowl and add the onion, green pepper, eggs, mustard, mayonnaise, dill, pepper, and the remaining 1 teaspoon of salt. Toss gently until well mixed, and transfer to the refrigerator for several hours. Serve chilled.

perfect hard-boiled eggs

When making hard-boiled eggs, contrary to what you may have been taught, it's best not to actually boil the eggs. The boiling process tends to crack the shells as a result of the eggs bumping into one another in the water. Instead, simmer the eggs just below the boiling point for 12 to 15 minutes. This will also reduce the risk of overcooking the white before the yolk is fully cooked (the white cooks before the yolk).

After cooking the eggs, remove them from the hot water and immerse them immediately in ice-cold water to halt the cooking process. This also helps to avoid the green color where the yolk meets the white of the egg.

Remove the eggs from the cold-water bath, crack the shells, and peel. Rinse once again with cold water to remove any small pieces of shell, and pat them dry.

grilled corn with lime juice

A Mexican friend recently served this corn to a group of friends at a dinner party in Sag Harbor. Everyone looked surprised when they were handed the freshly grilled corn with husks still on. But once they followed Ricardo's lead and pulled back the husks, and dressed the corn with the fresh lime and salt, no one could believe how delicious and refreshing it was. We all fought for the last ear.

8 ears of corn, husks intact	2 limes, quartered
	Salt, to taste

Open the husks and peel away from the cobs, but leave attached. Remove the silk from each ear, then push the husks back into place. Soak the de-silked corn in water for at least an hour before grilling; this helps the corn to cook thoroughly before charring on the grill.

Meanwhile, preheat a gas grill to medium-high or a charcoal grill until the embers are glowing.

Place the corn on the grill, turning frequently until the husks begin to char. Once the husks are thoroughly charred, remove from the grill to a large platter and serve immediately with wedges of lime and a dish of salt. The best way to eat this is to pull down the husks, remove any remaining silk, squeeze on the lime, sprinkle with salt, and enjoy.

the perfect ear of corn

Nothing defines summer as much as a simple ear of corn, slathered with butter and salt. Adding milk to the boiling water helps bring out the sweetness of the corn. Though everyone on the East End zealously buys corn all summer long, true die-hards wait until August for the perfect ear of sweet white corn. There's no comparison.

¼ cup whole milk	8 tablespoons (1 stick)	2 tablespoons salt
8 ears of corn, husked and	butter, melted	
silked		

fill a large pot with water and bring it to a rapid boil. Add the milk and corn and cook for 5 minutes, until the kernels are tender and juicy when pierced with a fork. Drain, transfer to a large platter, brush generously with the melted butter, sprinkle with salt, and serve.

baked rosemary potato chips

A great alternative to bagged chips, and almost as simple to pull together and serve to your guests. Try experimenting with different fresh herbs for a twist. Serve plain or with a favorite dip—we like Round Swamp Farm's onion dip or the sun-dried tomato dip from East Hampton's Barefoot Contessa.

½ cup olive oil, plus more for greasing the pan
3 pounds Idaho baking potatoes, peeled, rinsed, dried, and sliced ⅛ inch thick

2 to 3 tablespoons minced fresh rosemary

Salt and freshly ground black pepper, to taste

Preheat the oven to 475°F. and lightly grease a cookie sheet with olive oil.
  In a large bowl, toss the potatoes in the ½ cup of olive oil, then arrange the slices in a single layer on the prepared sheet. (The potatoes will need to be cooked in batches—they won't all fit on a single cookie sheet.) Sprinkle with the rosemary, salt, and pepper, and bake for 15 to 20 minutes, until crisp and golden brown. Remove from the oven and drain on paper towels. Season with additional salt and pepper if desired.

sugar snaps
with butter and chives

The crunchy, buttery, salty flavor of freshly picked sugar snap peas is truly the perfect additon to any summertime meal.

1 pound sugar snap peas, washed and ends snipped

4 tablespoons (½ stick) lightly salted butter, cut into 4 pieces

1 teaspoon salt
1 tablespoon finely chopped chives

bring 1½ cups of water to a boil. Using a double boiler or a vegetable steamer, steam the sugar snap peas until they turn a deep green, 2 to 3 minutes; do not overcook or they will immediately get mushy. Meanwhile, place the butter and salt in the bottom of a bowl. Immediately transfer the hot snap peas to the prepared bowl and stir, allowing the heat from the peas to melt the butter completely. Sprinkle on the chives before serving.

creamy coleslaw

The quintessential summer side dish—great with ribs, delicious with steamed lobster, ideal next to a sandwich. It's hard to go wrong with homemade coleslaw. We like to prepare it several hours in advance, giving the flavors a chance to marry.

½ head of red cabbage, rinsed and chopped

½ head of white cabbage, rinsed and chopped

½ cup Hellmann's mayonnaise

1½ teaspoons salt

1 tablespoon granulated sugar

Juice of 1 lemon (approximately ¼ cup)

In a large bowl, toss the red and white cabbage, mayonnaise, salt, sugar, and lemon juice until well combined. Refrigerate for several hours before serving.

grilled vegetables

A colorful side dish that makes a beautiful and healthful presentation.

1 cup extra-virgin olive oil
¼ cup balsamic vinegar
4 garlic cloves, minced
1 tablespoon minced fresh
   rosemary
½ teaspoon freshly ground
   black pepper, plus more
   to taste
1 tablespoon plus 1 teaspoon
   salt, plus more to taste

1 large green bell pepper,
   quartered and seeded
1 large red bell pepper,
   quartered and seeded
1 large yellow bell pepper,
   quartered and seeded
1 large yellow squash, sliced
   diagonally into ½-inch
   slices

1 large zucchini, sliced
   diagonally into ½-inch
   slices
2 large portobello
   mushrooms, brushed,
   cleaned, and stemmed
2 large Vidalia onions, sliced
   crosswise into ½-inch
   slices

Preheat a gas grill to medium-high heat or a charcoal grill so that the embers are glowing.

In a large bowl, combine the oil, vinegar, garlic, rosemary, pepper, and 1 teaspoon of salt. Whisk together and set aside.

Fill a large pot three-quarters full with water, add the remaining 1 tablespoon of salt, and bring to a rapid boil. Add the bell peppers and blanch for 3 to 5 minutes, until just tender when pierced. Remove from the water with a slotted spoon, and drain well. Repeat this procedure with the yellow squash and zucchini.

Toss all the vegetables in the marinade, coating well. Arrange the vegetables directly on the grill, and cook for the following times: peppers, squash, and zucchini for 3 to 6 minutes, until nicely charred; mushrooms for 6 to 8 minutes, until charred and tender; onions for 8 to 12 minutes, until charred and tender.

Baste the vegetables with the reserved marinade while cooking, turning frequently throughout. Once cooked, transfer to a large platter, sprinkle with salt and pepper to taste, and serve at room temperature.

savory watermelon salad

This unusual combination of flavors and textures makes a beautiful summer salad that is sweet, salty, soft, and crunchy all at the same time. It's a unique surprise for even the most seasoned palate.

1 3½-pound slice of watermelon, rind removed and chopped into 1- to 2-inch cubes (approximately 4 cups)

12 red radishes, washed and thinly sliced
½ pound feta cheese, crumbled
15 mint leaves, finely chopped

3 tablespoons balsamic vinegar
3 tablespoons extra-virgin olive oil

Combine the watermelon and radishes on a serving platter. Top with the feta cheese and mint. Drizzle with balsamic vinegar and olive oil, and serve.

asparagus with garlic and rosemary

A light and summery dish that complements almost any meal. We like to serve it alongside grilled fish or meat.

1½ teaspoons salt
2 bunches (approximately
 2 pounds) of asparagus,
 washed and trimmed
¼ cup extra-virgin olive oil

1 to 2 medium garlic cloves,
 minced
1 teaspoon finely chopped
 fresh rosemary

2 tablespoons fresh lemon
 juice (from about
 ½ lemon)
¼ teaspoon coarsely ground
 black pepper

fill a deep saucepan with approximately 2 inches of water, add 1 teaspoon of the salt, and bring to a rapid boil. Add the asparagus, bring to a second boil, then reduce the heat to low and simmer until the asparagus turn a deep green, 5 to 6 minutes. Drain the asparagus, rinse them with cold water, and drain again. Arrange in an oblong baking dish.

For the dressing, combine the oil, garlic, rosemary, lemon juice, the remaining ½ teaspoon of salt, and the pepper in a small bowl. Let the dressing sit at room temperature for 15 to 20 minutes for the flavors to marry. Drizzle the dressing over the asparagus, toss gently, and marinate for approximately 30 minutes. Serve at room temperature.

roasted tomatoes and garlic

These tomatoes can stand on their own or can be used to liven up pasta or even a sandwich.

10 plum tomatoes, rinsed, halved lengthwise, tops removed

⅓ cup olive oil

1 head of garlic, separated into cloves with skin intact

1 tablespoon salt

1 teaspoon freshly ground black pepper

Preheat the oven to 350°F.

In a bowl, toss the tomatoes with the olive oil, garlic, salt, and pepper. Place the tomatoes, cut-side down, on a cookie sheet lined with aluminum foil, and place the garlic in the empty spaces among the tomatoes. Pour any remaining oil, salt, and pepper over the tomatoes and garlic. Roast for 20 minutes, or until the tomato skins begin to loosen. Remove from the oven, peel away the skins, and discard. Lower the oven temperature to 275°F. Drain any liquid from the pan and return to the oven for 2 to 3 hours, until the tomatoes are shriveled, periodically removing any liquid from the pan. Before serving, remove the garlic flesh from the skins.

drinks

Homemade Berry-Citrus Iced Tea

Fresh Strawberry-Mint Lemonade

Limeade

Southside

Margarita

Bloody Mary

homemade berry-citrus iced tea

This refreshing summer drink is delicious on its own, or mixed with fresh lemonade (half and half) to make an Arnold Palmer.

1 quart boiling water
8 tea bags of mango or other fruit-infused black tea
1½ quarts cold filtered water

⅔ cup superfine sugar
½ cup blueberries
½ cup raspberries
4 to 6 large strawberries, hulled and sliced

1 navel orange, quartered
1 lemon, quartered

In a large pitcher, pour the boiling water over the tea bags and let steep for 4 to 5 minutes. Remove the tea bags and add the cold water, sugar, berries, orange, and lemon and stir until well mixed. Refrigerate until cold (the longer the tea sits, the more flavorful it becomes) and serve in a tall glass over ice, fruit and all.

flavored ice cubes

The trick to keeping your summer drinks from getting watery is to make ice cubes that won't turn into water when they melt. We like to freeze tea and coffee to keep these drinks strong, and we like to chill lemonade by using frozen fruit instead of ice cubes. Frozen fruit is also helpful when making smoothies, so you don't need to add any ice.

fresh strawberry-mint lemonade

PHOTOGRAPHS ON PAGES 110-111

For those looking for a simpler lemonade, just omit the strawberry purée or mint leaves from the following recipe. You might wish to add a little more sugar if the strawberry purée is not added, as the lemonade will be slightly more tart.

6 lemons, juiced to yield 1
    cup lemon juice
¾ to 1 cup superfine sugar,
    to taste
1½ quarts filtered water

1 pint (approximately 10)
    large strawberries, hulled,
    plus more for garnish
    (optional)

1 small bunch of mint leaves
    (approximately ½ cup),
    plus more for garnish
    (optional)
1 lemon, sliced, for garnish
    (optional)

In a large pitcher, combine the lemon juice, sugar, and water, and stir until well mixed. Using a blender or food processor, purée the strawberries, and add to the lemonade mixture along with the mint leaves. Stir well once again, and refrigerate until cold.

Serve in a tall glass over ice, garnished with a slice of lemon and a small strawberry or mint sprig.

RIGHT AND OPPOSITE: Fresh Strawberry-Mint
Lemonade (recipe on page 109).

limeade

This refreshing alternative to the more traditional lemonade is also great served as a citrus spritzer with sparkling water added to taste.

12 limes, juiced to yield
  1½ cups lime juice, plus
  2 limes, quartered, for
  garnish

½ cup superfine sugar
1 quart filtered water

In a large pitcher, combine the lime juice, sugar, and water, and stir until well mixed. Refrigerate until chilled. Serve in a tall glass over ice with a slice of lime as a garnish.

southside

We always know it's summer when our friend Tim Bogardus starts mixing the Southsides. Lemonade with a kick, it's so hard to have just one, we usually make a pitcher and plan to spend the whole evening at home.

1 heaping tablespoon superfine sugar
1 lemon, juiced
3 to 5 spearmint leaves, roughly torn

Crushed or cracked ice (to fill a tumbler)
1 to 2 jiggers dry gin
Splash of club soda (optional)

Thinly sliced lemon, for garnish
Mint sprig, for garnish

Using a tumbler, dissolve the sugar in the lemon juice and 1 tablespoon of water. Add the spearmint, and muddle in the bottom of the glass until the oil is released from the mint and the mixture becomes fragrant. Fill a glass with crushed or cracked ice (do not use large ice cubes) and pour in the gin. For a lighter drink, add club soda. Stir until thoroughly chilled, garnish with a lemon slice and mint sprig, and serve.

margarita

The fresh lime juice and Cointreau are what really make this margarita—courtesy of Della Femina restaurant bartender Bob Barzilay—extra special.

15 ounces (just under 2 cups) best-quality tequila

3 ounces sour mix

3 ounces fresh lime juice (from about 4 limes)

3 ounces Cointreau

3 ounces orange juice (from about 2 oranges)

Kosher salt

1 lime, quartered, for salting the rim, plus 1½ limes, quartered, for garnish

In a large pitcher, combine the tequila, sour mix, lime juice, Cointreau, and orange juice. Mix well. Spread the salt on a plate. Moisten the rim of a highball or snifter glass with one of the pieces of lime, and dip the rim in the plate of salt. Fill the glass with ice and the margarita mixture and garnish with lime.

bloody mary

Using salt on the rim of the glass, lots of fresh horseradish, and lemon- or pepper-flavored vodka are the secrets—courtesy of bartender Bob Barzilay—of this delicious cocktail, perfect at any time of day.

1 46-ounce can of
Sacramento tomato juice
2 limes, juiced, to yield
2 tablespoons fresh lime
juice plus 1 lime,
quartered, for salting
the rim

3 tablespoons prepared
horseradish
2 tablespoons Tabasco sauce
4 tablespoons
Worcestershire sauce
1 teaspoon freshly ground
black pepper

22½ ounces (just under
3 cups) vodka, preferably
pepper- or citrus-flavored
Kosher salt
Celery, for garnish

In a large pitcher, combine the tomato juice, lime juice, horseradish, Tabasco, Worcestershire, and pepper. Mix well.

Fill a shaker with ice and add 2½ ounces of vodka and 5 ounces of the tomato juice mixture and shake well. Spread the salt on a plate. Moisten the rim of a highball or snifter glass with one of the pieces of lime and dip the rim in a plate of salt. Pour the bloody mary into the glass and garnish with a rib of celery.

desserts

s'mores

One of our favorite summer desserts, delicious after a barbecue or at a late-night bonfire on the beach. Be sure to collect plenty of sticks and branches before the sun goes down, so that you can authentically toast the perfect marshmallow.

12 marshmallows

6 graham crackers, each split in half to make a total of 12 squares

2 Hershey chocolate bars, each broken in 3 pieces

evenly toast 2 marshmallows at a time until golden brown. Lay out 6 of the 12 graham cracker squares, and place one third of a chocolate bar on each square. As soon as the marshmallow is sufficiently browned and heated through, place it on top of the chocolate, and use the remaining 6 graham cracker squares to make 6 "sandwiches." Apply light pressure on each so that the heat from the marshmallow melts the chocolate.

summer fruit salad

One of the best things about summer is the beautiful, ripe fruit overflowing from every farm stand on the East End. A fruit salad filled with color (and an absence of any fruit that turns brown) seems almost too good to be true. The cranberries add a simple tartness, while the mint just adds the flavor of pure summer.

3 plums, pitted and cubed
3 peaches, pitted and cubed
3 white peaches, pitted and cubed
2 cups cherries, stemmed and pitted

1 cup raspberries
1 cup blueberries
1½ cups strawberries, stemmed and sliced
1½ cups green (or red) grapes

1 cup dried cranberries
½ cup orange juice
1 bunch of mint, stemmed and thinly sliced

In a large bowl, combine all the ingredients. Mix well and refrigerate until ready to serve.

grilled summer fruit

Grilling fruit is a great way to end any summer meal. Be sure to clean off your grill well so that the flavors from dinner don't taint the sweet ending to your evening. We like to add Devonshire Cream, a thick clotted cream from Devonshire, England.

½ cup honey
½ cup brown sugar, plus more for garnish
1 teaspoon pure vanilla extract

½ cup balsamic vinegar
3 ripe peaches, pitted and halved
3 ripe white peaches, pitted and halved

3 ripe nectarines, pitted and halved
6 thick pineapple slices
¾ to 1 cup Devonshire cream

Preheat a gas grill to medium-high or a charcoal grill until the embers are glowing.

In a small bowl, whisk together the honey, sugar, vanilla, and vinegar. Soak the fruit in the mixture for 10 to 15 minutes while the grill heats up, then transfer the fruit to the grill, brushing the remaining marinade on the fruit as it cooks (turning once or twice) for 4 to 5 minutes. Remove from the grill, and serve topped with a large dollop of Devonshire cream and a sprinkle of brown sugar.

single pie crust

The essential part of every summer pie starts with the crust, and we have found that the key comes from mixing shortening and butter.

1¼ cups all-purpose presifted flour	⅓ cup shortening	1 to 2 tablespoons ice-cold water
½ teaspoon salt	2 tablespoons unsalted butter	

In a medium bowl, combine the flour and salt. Using a pastry blender or two knives, cut in the shortening and butter until the mixture resembles small peas or gravel. Sprinkle with cold water (1 tablespoon at a time), tossing lightly and stirring with a fork. (Add each tablespoon of water to the driest part of the mixture.) The dough should be moist enough to hold together when pressed gently with a fork, but it should not be too sticky.

Shape the dough into a smooth ball, and refrigerate for 1 to 2 hours. Roll out on a lightly floured surface, rolling the dough from the center out in all directions to ⅛ inch thickness, making a 10- to 11-inch circle. Then fold the dough in half, and ease it loosely into the pie pan with a fold in the center. Gently press out any air pockets with your fingertips and be sure that there are no openings for any filling to escape. Fold under the edge of the crust and press into the pie rim. Crimp the edges as desired, and refrigerate until ready to fill.

To prebake the pie shell, preheat the oven to 450°F. Prepare as directed above, then prick the bottom and sides of the shell evenly and closely with a 4-tined fork. Line the pie shell with wax paper, fill the shell with pastry weights or dry beans, and bake in the preheated oven for 10 to 15 minutes, or until lightly brown. Remove from the oven and cool before filling.

double pie crust

3 cups all-purpose presifted
  flour
1½ teaspoons salt

¾ cup shortening
¼ cup plus 2 tablespoons
  unsalted butter

6 tablespoons ice-cold water

In a medium bowl, combine the flour and salt. Using a pastry blender or two knives, cut in the shortening and butter until the mixture resembles small peas or gravel. Sprinkle with cold water (1 tablespoon at a time), tossing lightly and stirring with a fork. (Add each tablespoon of water to the driest part of the mixture.) The dough should be moist enough to hold together when pressed gently with a fork, but it should not be too sticky.

Divide the dough into two equal balls, and refrigerate for 1 to 2 hours. Roll one of the balls out on a lightly floured surface, rolling the dough from the center out in all directions to ⅛ inch thickness, making a 10- to 11-inch circle. Then fold the dough in half, and ease it loosely into the pie pan with a fold in the center. Gently press out any air pockets with your fingertips and be sure that there are no openings for any filling to escape.

Add the filling, following recipe directions. Then roll out the top crust following the same directions. Place it on top, and trim and crimp the edges of the pie shell. Cut slits in the top crust to allow any steam to escape. Bake as directed.

triple-berry pie

The secret to this mixed-berry pie is the addition of rose water, an aromatic exotic flavoring made from pure extract of rose. Available at most gourmet and specialty stores, rose water is perfect with any fruit; we like to add it to homemade jam, fruit salad, and of course fruit pies. This pie can be made with any combination of berries, and it's best when it's topped with a scoop of vanilla ice cream or a dollop of Devonshire cream.

2 cups fresh blueberries, stemmed
2 cups fresh raspberries
2 cups fresh blackberries
1¼ cups sugar
¼ cup flour

2 tablespoons fresh lemon juice (from about ½ lemon)
1 teaspoon rose water (optional)
2 teaspoons ground cinnamon

1 Double Pie Crust (page 125)
1 tablespoon lightly salted butter, cut into small pieces

Preheat the oven to 375°F.

Combine the blueberries, raspberries, and blackberries in a large bowl. Add the sugar, flour, lemon juice, rose water, and cinnamon, and mix well. Pour the filling into the bottom of the prepared pie shell, and sprinkle small pieces of butter on top. Apply the top crust, seal the edges, and using a sharp knife, make three slits in the center of the pie to vent the steam. Bake for 50 to 60 minutes, until the crust is golden brown. Remove from the oven and let sit at room temperature until the pie is cool. Serve with your favorite topping.

apple pie

Everyone has a favorite version. We like to serve it warm, with a decadent dollop of Devonshire cream on top.

8 medium Granny Smith apples (3 to 3½ pounds), peeled, cored, and sliced ⅛ inch thick
1 cup granulated sugar
⅓ cup plus 2 tablespoons firmly packed brown sugar
1½ tablespoons ground cinnamon
¼ teaspoon salt
3 tablespoons all-purpose flour
1 Double Pie Crust (page 125)
1 tablespoon unsalted butter, cut into small pieces

Preheat the oven to 375°F.

In a large bowl, combine the apples, sugars, cinnamon, salt, and flour, and toss until the apples are well coated. Pour the apple mixture into the bottom crust, and sprinkle evenly with the butter.

Place the top crust over the apples, trim and crimp the edges, and cut slits in the top crust for steam to escape. Bake for 50 minutes, or until the crust is golden brown and the filling bubbles. Serve warm or at room temperature.

pecan pie

This nougat-filled pie is for anyone with a sweet tooth that can barely be satiated. Sometimes, just to cover all the bases, we like to add some milk-chocolate chips before pouring the batter into the pie shell. Make sure to prepare this well in advance, especially on a hot summer day, because it needs several hours to set.

3 eggs, lightly beaten
1 cup dark Karo syrup
1 cup sugar
2 tablespoons (¼ stick) salted butter, melted

½ teaspoon pure almond extract
½ teaspoon pure vanilla extract
2 cups chopped pecans

1 Single Pie Crust (page 124), not blind-baked

Preheat the oven to 350°F.

Mix the eggs and the Karo syrup together in a large bowl, then add the sugar and mix well. Add the melted butter and extracts, and stir to combine. Add the chopped pecans and mix thoroughly, until all the pecans are covered in syrup. Pour the mixture into the unbaked pie shell.

Bake for 1 hour, or until the pie is golden brown and firm in the middle. Remove from the oven and cool at least 2 hours before serving.

strawberry-rhubarb pie

A big seller on the East End throughout the summer season, strawberry-rhubarb is the perfect balance of tart and sweet when freshly grown stalks of rhubarb meet handpicked sugary strawberries. We like to serve ours with vanilla ice cream, whipped cream, or crème fraîche.

1 Double Pie Crust (page 125)
3½ cups rhubarb, sliced ½ inch thick

3½ cups strawberries, hulled and sliced ½ inch thick
2 cups granulated sugar
⅔ cup all-purpose flour

2 teaspoons ground cinnamon
½ teaspoon salt
2 tablespoons unsalted butter, cut into small cubes

Preheat the oven to 375° F.

Place the bottom crust in a pie pan, trim the edges, pierce the bottom with a fork, and refrigerate. Roll out the top crust, place on a cookie sheet, and refrigerate. Both the bottom and top crusts should be refrigerated for 30 minutes.

In a medium bowl, combine the rhubarb, strawberries, sugar, flour, cinnamon, and salt, and toss until well blended. Pour the mixture into the bottom crust, and top evenly with the butter. Fold the top crust in half, place it on one side of the pie, and unfold it to cover the rest of the pie. Trim and crimp the edges together, and cut slits in the top to allow steam to escape. Transfer to the preheated oven and bake for 50 to 60 minutes, or until the crust is golden brown and the filling is bubbling. Remove from the oven and cool on a wire rack for several hours. Serve at room temperature.

key lime–meringue pie

Though key-lime pie is traditionally made from the juice of tart key limes, we have found that regular limes make a great substitute in a pinch. Whichever lime you choose, use the same amount, and don't be surprised by the light yellow color of this dessert: The green key-lime pies you may be more used to get their deep hue from food coloring, not fresh lime juice. This pie is also great when it's made with a graham cracker crust, and it's always delicious topped with a spoonful of fresh whipped cream and garnished with thinly sliced limes.

for the pie
⅓ cup plus 1 tablespoon
   cornstarch
1½ cups sugar
¼ teaspoon salt
3 egg yolks, beaten

2 tablespoons lime zest
¼ cup fresh lime juice (from
   3 to 4 limes)
1 Single Pie Crust, prebaked
   and cooled (page 124)

for the meringue topping
4 egg whites, at room
   temperature
¼ teaspoon salt
¼ teaspoon cream of tartar
¼ teaspoon pure vanilla
   extract
½ cup sugar

Preheat the oven to 350°F.

In a medium saucepan, combine the cornstarch, sugar, and salt. Add 1½ cups water and stir constantly over medium heat until the mixture comes to a boil. Remove the pan from the heat. Add a few tablespoons of the hot mixture to the egg yolks, then place the egg-yolk mixture back into the saucepan and mix thoroughly. Bring the mixture to a second boil over medium heat, stirring constantly. Boil for 1 minute, and remove the pan from the heat. Stir in the lime zest and juice, and pour into the prepared pie shell.

In a medium bowl, combine the egg whites, salt, cream of tartar, and vanilla. Using an electric mixer, beat at medium speed until the entire mixture is frothy but not stiff. Add the sugar, a little bit at a time, beating well after each addition. Beat until all of the sugar dissolves (do not underbeat). Continue beating until the egg whites are stiff and peaks form when you slowly lift the beater.

Spoon the meringue around the edge of the pie filling; be sure that the meringue touches the inner edge of the crust to avoid shrinkage of the meringue. Pile the remaining meringue in the center of the pie, and spread it to meet the meringue around the edges. Bake for 10 to 15 minutes, until the meringue is golden brown. Transfer to a wire rack (away from any drafts), and let cool for at least 1 hour before cutting.

raspberry peach cobbler

Round Swamp Farm is a favorite of many on the East End for the wonderful produce grown out back. Lisa, the daughter of owner Carolyn Snyder, has been baking Round Swamp's goodies since she was nine. She rarely parts with a recipe, so this recipe of hers is a treat.

6 cups ripe peaches, peeled, pitted, and sliced
1½ tablespoons plus ½ teaspoon lemon juice (from about 1 lemon)
¾ cup plus 2 tablespoons sugar

2¼ cups plus 1 tablespoon all-purpose flour
2 teaspoons ground cinnamon
2 cups ripe raspberries
1¼ teaspoons baking powder

½ teaspoon salt
½ cup (1 stick) unsalted butter, chilled and cut into small pieces
¼ cup whole milk
2 large eggs

Preheat the oven to 350°F.

In a large bowl, toss the peaches with 1½ tablespoons of the lemon juice. Combine ¾ cup of sugar, ¼ cup of flour, and the cinnamon. Add this to the peach mixture, and toss lightly. Spread the mixture in a deep baking pan and set aside.

In a medium bowl, toss the raspberries with the remaining ½ teaspoon of lemon juice. Combine 2 tablespoons sugar and 1 tablespoon flour. Add to the raspberries, and toss. Gently add the raspberry mixture to the peach mixture by placing dollops of raspberry around the dish. Place in the preheated oven and bake until the mixture bubbles, about 20 minutes.

Using a food processor, combine the baking powder, salt, butter, the remaining 2 cups of flour, and salt. Pulse until crumbly. Don't overprocess or the mixture will get tough. Transfer to a medium bowl, and make a well in the center. In a small bowl, whisk together the milk and eggs. Add this to the flour mixture, cutting it into the mix with a fork until slightly moist.

Sprinkle the crumble mixture on top of the bubbling fruit and return to the oven. Bake until the top is golden brown, about 25 minutes.

blondies

The Heath Bar candy bits really make these special, a great treat for those who haven't outgrown their childhood sweet tooth.

1 cup (2 sticks) unsalted butter, softened, plus more for greasing the pan
2½ cups all-purpose flour
1½ teaspoons baking powder
½ teaspoon salt

1½ cups firmly packed dark brown sugar
2 jumbo eggs
1 teaspoon vanilla extract
1 teaspoon almond extract
1 cup semisweet chocolate chips

2 teaspoons cinnamon
½ cup walnuts
½ cup raisins
½ cup shredded coconut
½ cup Heath Bar bits

Preheat the oven to 350°F. Grease a 13 × 9 × 2-inch baking dish with butter.

In a medium bowl, combine the flour, baking powder, and salt. In a separate bowl, cream together the cup of butter and the sugar, then add the eggs and vanilla and almond extracts. Slowly combine with the flour mixture, and add the chocolate chips, cinnamon, walnuts, raisins, coconut, and Heath Bar bits. Mix until all of the ingredients are well blended.

Fold the batter into the prepared baking dish and bake for 40 minutes, until golden brown. Allow to cool for at least 1 hour, then cut into squares and serve.

lemon cake squares

This dessert is great served after a seafood meal. These lemon cake squares are a light and tart variation on lemon curd squares, making them difficult to pass up even when dessert sounds too decadent. They're especially tempting when cut into small squares and presented on a platter with fresh berries and a sprinkle of confectioners' sugar.

1¼ cups all-purpose flour
1 teaspoon baking powder
½ teaspoon salt
½ cup (1 stick) unsalted butter, softened, plus more for greasing the pan

1 cup sugar
2 jumbo eggs, lightly beaten
½ cup whole milk
2 tablespoons grated lemon zest

6 tablespoons fresh lemon juice (from about 4 lemons)
1½ cup sifted confectioners' sugar

Preheat the oven to 350°F. Butter an 8 × 8 × 2-inch baking pan.

In a medium bowl, combine the flour, baking powder, and salt and set aside. In a large bowl, cream the ½ cup of butter and the sugar together, then add the eggs, milk, lemon zest, and 3 tablespoons of the lemon juice; stir to combine. Add the dry ingredients to this mixture and stir until the batter is smooth. Pour into the prepared pan and bake for 40 minutes, or until a toothpick inserted into the middle of the cake comes out clean.

Meanwhile, prepare the syrup: Whisk together the confectioners' sugar and the remaining 3 tablespoons of lemon juice.

Remove the cake from the oven, pour the syrup over the top, and spread evenly. Cool on a wire rack, then cut into squares.

almond cake
with raspberry sauce

This cake is simple in both preparation and presentation. Served with a delicate topping of home-made raspberry sauce, this dessert has a bright, no-fuss quality that defines summer at the beach.

¾ cup (1½ sticks) unsalted butter, softened, plus more for greasing the pan
10½ ounces marzipan

4 jumbo eggs
2 teaspoons almond extract
1 cup sugar
⅛ teaspoon salt

¾ cup cake flour
⅔ cup coconut flakes
1 pint fresh raspberries

Preheat the oven to 350°F. Grease a 10-inch springform pan.

In a large bowl, combine the ¾ cup butter and the marzipan and blend with a hand mixer on medium speed until well mixed. Add the eggs one at a time, blending after each addition. Add the almond extract, ½ cup of the sugar, the salt, and cake flour, and beat on medium speed until well blended, scraping any excess off the sides of the bowl.

Pour the batter into the prepared pan and sprinkle the coconut flakes over the top. Bake for 40 to 45 minutes, until a toothpick inserted in the middle comes out clean.

Meanwhile, combine the raspberries and the remaining ½ cup of sugar in a small saucepan and bring to a rapid boil. Reduce the heat to low and simmer for 2 to 3 minutes, stirring constantly. Remove from the heat and let cool to room temperature.

When both the cake and syrup have cooled to room temperature, slice the almond cake, and serve it topped with raspberry syrup.

marzipan vs. almond paste

Marzipan has significantly more sugar than almond paste, but the two are nearly interchangeable, and one can be substituted for the other in a pinch.

an enormous thank you to everyone who helped

us to create this book, especially our tasting crew—Carl, Ian, Daniel, Sean, Jordan, Marcia, John, Evelyn, Yon, Andrew, Daniel, Karen, Chester, and Henry —you never seemed to tire of our seemingly endless meals; to everyone at the Lobster Roll for your hard work, support, and incredible loyalty, with special thanks to twenty-year manager, Paul DeAngelis, and his incredible managerial staff—Glen Bazazian, Richie Einslider, John Fondrisi, Tim Haberstumf, Walter Hardy, Sebastian Pulido, and Carol Slattery; to the wonderful professional and recreational chefs and bartenders who continue to inspire us, and who are always generous in sharing their culinary secrets and expertise—Bob Barzilay, David Bernier, Tim Bogardus, the Della Femina family, Lisa Niggles Snyder, Susan Pardo, Rebecca Rubel, Maureen Theard, and Jennifer Theard; to Ben Fink for sharing his remarkable photographic talent—working together was truly a treat; and, of course, we can't thank enough the entire Round Swamp family and Charlotte and Bruce Sasso of Stuart's Seafood Market for giving us hours of incredible things to shoot—Charlotte, you proved to be an endless source of information up to the last possible minute, and we thank you profusely for your help; to Heather Schroder, our fabulous agent at ICM; to Chris Pavone, our wonderful editor at Clarkson Potter—without you this book wouldn't exist; to the production editor, Mark McCauslin, the production supervisor, Alison Forner, and the creator of the beautiful design, Jane Treuhaft; and finally to Fred Terry and the entire Terry family, for without them, there would be no Lobster Roll, and summer just wouldn't be the same. Thank you!

equivalent imperial and metric measurements

American cooks use standard containers, the 8-ounce cup and a tablespoon that takes exactly 16 level fillings to fill that cup level. Measuring by cup makes it very difficult to give weight equivalents, as a cup of densely packed butter will weigh considerably more than a cup of flour. The easiest way therefore to deal with cup measurements in recipes is to take the amount by volume rather than by weight. Thus the equation reads:

1 cup = 240 ml = 8 fl. oz.   ½ cup = 120 ml = 4 fl. oz.

In the States, butter is often measured in sticks. One stick is the equivalent of 8 tablespoons. One tablespoon of butter is therefore the equivalent to ½ ounce/15 grams.

SOLID MEASURES

U.S. and Imperial Measures		Metric Measures	
Ounces	*Pounds*	*Grams*	*Kilos*
1		28	
2		56	
3½		100	
4	¼	112	
5		140	
6		168	
8	½	225	
9		250	¼
12	¾	340	
16	1	450	
18		500	½

LIQUID MEASURES

Fluid Ounces	*U.S.*	*Imperial*	*Milliliters*
	1 teaspoon	1 teaspoon	5
¼	2 teaspoons	1 dessertspoon	10
½	1 tablespoon	1 tablespoon	14
1	2 tablespoons	2 tablespoons	28
2	¼ cup	4 tablespoons	56
4	½ cup		120
5		¼ pint or 1 gill	140
6	¾ cup		170
8	1 cup		240
9			250, ¼ liter
10	1¼ cups	½ pint	280
12	1½ cups		340
15		¾ pint	420
16	2 cups		450

OVEN TEMPERATURE EQUIVALENTS

Fahrenheit	*Celsius*	*Gas Mark*	*Description*
225	110	¼	Cool
250	130	½	
275	140	1	Very Slow
300	150	2	
325	170	3	Slow
350	180	4	Moderate
375	190	5	
400	200	6	Moderately Hot
425	220	7	Fairly Hot
450	230	8	Hot
475	240	9	Very Hot
500	250	10	Extremely Hot

Any broiling recipes can be used with the grill of the oven, but beware of high-temperature grills.

EQUIVALENTS FOR INGREDIENTS AND TOOLS

all-purpose flour—plain flour
baking sheet—oven tray
buttermilk—ordinary milk
cheesecloth—muslin
coarse salt—kitchen salt
cornstarch—cornflour
eggplant—aubergine

granulated sugar—caster sugar
half and half—12% fat milk
heavy cream—double cream
light cream—single cream
lima beans—broad beans
parchment paper—greaseproof paper
plastic wrap—cling film

scallion—spring onion
shortening—white fat
unbleached flour—strong, white flour
vanilla bean—vanilla pod
zest—rind
zucchini—courgettes or marrow